THE STORY OF
NORMANTON

THE STORY OF NORMANTON

Compiled by Members of the Normanton-by-Derby Local History Group & Friends

Contributors
Ron Adamson
Audrey Bate
Norma Consterdine
Leslie Cox
Phyllis Oldknow
Joyce Poynton
Judith Raven
Michael Shaw
Peter & Eileen Thompson

The Breedon Books
Publishing Company
Derby

First published in Great Britain by
The Breedon Books Publishing Company Limited
44 Friar Gate, Derby, DE1 1DA
1993

ISBN 1 873626 56 8

Printed and bound by Hillmans Printers, Frome, Somerset.
Covers printed by BDC Printing Services Limited of Derby.

Contents

Acknowledgements

The Normanton-by-Derby Local History Group wishes to express its thanks to all who have provided photographs and material for this book, including Mrs G.Cheetham, the Cooper family, Mr Leslie Cox, Mrs Cresswell, Mr Bernard Diver, the family of the late Miss Irene Draper, Mr Stan Fletcher, Connie Handley, Mr A.Hawksworth, Miss Kathleen Louch, Mrs May Savage, Mrs Betty Spencer, Mrs Monica Swinburn for the use of the late Mr Joe Harrison's photographs, Miss Kitty Wallace, Mr E.Wheatley (photographs of Old Hall Farm), NEI International Combustion Ltd, Reckitt & Colman Ltd (F.W.Hampshire), W & J Richardson Ltd, White Bros (Derby) Ltd, Derby Local Studies Library, Derby Museum, the staff of the Mayor's office, *Derby Evening Telegraph*, Normanton Infant, Normanton Village Infant, Junior and Village Community Schools and all those who provided reminiscences.

Special mention must also be made of the invaluable help provided by the late Mr Joe Harrison's *Some Account of Normanton-by-Derby and its Church*.

Whilst every effort has been made to be as accurate as possible, with the material available, the Group would be glad to know if readers have anything to add or have more stories about Normanton.

Dedicated to the Revd Canon Barrie Blowers,
Vicar of Normanton-by-Derby 1969-1993,
whose vision for the
Normanton Local History Festival in May 1992
provided the impetus for this book.

Foreword

SUBURBS are not thought to be interesting. They are, after all, only the middle-age spread of a town and do no more for a place than for a person. Well, that is the way the conventional mind works, but it is not necessarily true. Certainly it isn't entirely true of suburban Derby. A few early inner suburbs, admittedly, were protrudences from the core of the ancient borough, but their growth was usually blocked by the presence of some prosperous private estate. A mile or so beyond these was a ring of ancient rural villages, each with a life of its own and not looking particularly to Derby before the 19th century. These are now the city's outer suburbs. Between these and the earliest bulge were built at varying periods large groups of houses forming what we should now call housing estates but what at the time were virtually new villages in their own right.

Normanton is an amalgam of both these last forms of development. The original Normanton-by-Derby (to distinguish it from Temple and South Normanton) was the ancient *Norse man's tun* or farm, created by invaders from Northern Europe. By 1877, it was a rural parish in the South Derbyshire Parliamentary constituency and in the hundred of Repton and Gresley. It lay two miles south of Derby railway station and had a population of 638. But in that year was grafted on to it New Normanton, one of those 'new villages'. The book that follows, planned, researched and written by members of the Normanton Local History Group, deals with the community that sprang out of this strange partnership.

One story, modestly understated in the book, seems to sum up the spirit of this community. Early in 1992, the then incumbent, Canon Barrie Blowers, suggested staging a Normanton Local History Festival. The Festival was held in May 1992, after an enthusiastic band of people had collected together a vast amount of material, written, spoken and in pictures. The sequel was the formation of the Normanton Local History Group, and the sequel to that, produced with quite astonishing speed, is this book.

You will enjoy it, I am sure, especially if you have any link with Normanton. It seems to me to be a model of its kind.

ROY CHRISTIAN MBE
Derby
September 1993

The Early History

THE Normanton Estate is situated in an excellent and rapidly improving neighbourhood . . .It is intersected by excellent Roads, and for a considerable distance by the Derby and Birmingham Railway: and the Railway about to be made from Derby to Melbourne is intended to pass through part of the Estate.

The Estate is celebrated for its healthy and commanding situation and it abounds with beautiful views of the surrounding and distant scenery: there are also numerous sites of the finest description for the erection of villas and first-class residences, and a portion of the land might be readily made available for other building purposes. Whether in a residential or commercial point of view, the Property will be found to offer advantages rarely to be met with.

Sale Notice 1865.

NORMANTON'S situation, about one and a half miles south of Derby on a ridge overlooking the Trent Valley, provided the Viking invaders of the ninth century with an ideal place for fortifications to protect their newly-conquered area of present-day Derby. Guthrum, a Danish chieftain, had brought his great army through the Kingdom of Mercia, up the River Trent, sacking villages and burning down Repton monastery and thus Normanton was founded and took its name 'the Northmen's town'.

In 917, however, Ethelfreda, daughter of King Alfred, bravely led the reorganised Saxon army up the slopes of Normanton from the Trent Valley, overpowered the Danish defenders and went on to retake the town of Northworthy, as Derby was then known.

Whether there was a settlement at Normanton before this we do not know, but historians are of the opinion that the estates of earlier ruling tribes formed the basis of subsequent settlements. In this case, the area where Normanton emerged could have been part of a large tract of land forming an estate which was in the possession of successive invaders from the time of the Coritani, a Celtic tribe known to have been living in middle England from at least Roman times, onwards.

By the time the Domesday Book was compiled, Derby was populated by a mixture of Saxons and Danes now under the rule of the Norman King, William the Conqueror.

The entry for Normanton reads: *In Normanton (-by Derby) Leofric, Gamel and Theodric had 6 bovates of land taxable. Land for 1 plough. Now in lordship 1 plough. 1 villager pays 12d. Meadow, 12 acres: a little underwood. Value before 1066, 20s now 10s. Almeric holds it. There are also 2 bovates of land taxable belonging to Twyford.*

There is an additional entry for Normanton under Melbourne as follows: *In Normanton (by Derby). 1 carucate land for 12 ploughs. Taxable 8 carucates and 2 bovates. (A bovate was a measure of land — as much as an ox team could plough in a year. Eight bovates were usually said to make a carucate).*

The main entry showed that it had previously been held by three people, Leofric, Gamel and Theodric, but was then held by Almeric under the Norman knight, Henry de Ferrers. Although only one villager, paying 12 pence, was mentioned, there may well have been others who paid tax to their local lord rather than to the king and so were not mentioned in the record. The above entries have been taken from the Phillimore edition of the Domesday Book which does not mention a church at Normanton. The statement that there was a church and two mills here contained in *The Domesday Book, England's Heritage, Then and Now*, edited by Thomas Hinde, seems to indicate that the information for another place called Normanton was mistakenly shown against Normanton-by-Derby.

By the end of the thirteenth century, the Canons of Darley Abbey had become the largest landholders in the village. They had built themselves a grange (an outlying farmhouse belonging to the monastery) and had built or re-built the church, but their influence in Normanton came to an end with the Dissolution of the Monasteries in 1538. There is no record of what the abbey's buildings here were like and they were demolished in due course. Perhaps the materials were used to build the Manor House which itself was said to be in a ruinous condition in 1712. It is tempting to assume that the Grange Hotel stands on the site of the monks' grange, but no evidence has been found to support this. The site of the Manor House is also waiting to be discovered.

In 1544, King Henry VIII granted the Manor of Normanton to Roland Babington who was connected with the Babingtons of Dethick in Derbyshire. A well-known member of that family, Anthony Babington, was executed for high treason for his involvement in a plot to put Mary, Queen of Scots, on the throne of England.

The estate was acquired in 1584 by Francis Beaumont, a judge, whose family came to England in the early fourteenth century and became connected by marriage with the reigning royal family. His home was at Grace Dieu in Leicestershire, where he died in 1598. His eldest son, Henry, who inherited the

Village Street, Normanton, looking east in the late nineteenth century. The ancient cottages in front of the churchyard were later demolished. Ivanhoe Terrace, at the corner of Browning Street, has not yet been built. The figures are Mr Brownsword, the verger, and his wife. The photograph was taken by Richard Keene.

Normanton estate, was knighted in 1603. Sir John, the second son, was a poet, and Francis, the third son, was a celebrated dramatic writer and is buried in Westminster Abbey.

After Sir Henry Beaumont died, his young widow, Lady Barbara Beaumont, married Sir Henry Harpur who was to purchase the Calke Abbey estate in 1622. They appear to have been living in Normanton in 1623. In 1645, during the Civil War, Lady Barbara presented Normanton Church with a silver chalice and paten, one of the very few to be made at this time. This gift, coming in the year of the forcible suppression of the Prayer Book, reflects the Royalist sympathies of the family at the time. Her daughter, also named Barbara, inherited the Normanton estate from her father and she married Sir John Harpur, a nephew of Sir Henry Harpur. Sir John died soon after their marriage and her second husband was Sir Woolstan Dixie of Market Bosworth. They seem to have been living in Normanton in 1655, when Sir Woolstan was fined heavily for supporting the Royalists in the Civil War.

When Sir Henry Beaumont died in 1605, a map of Normanton was made which listed the names of tenants and cottagers, showing each man's strips of cultivation in the common fields. One of the names, Tabberer, has been known in Normanton right up to the present day. As was usual at this time, farmhouses were built along the village street, although their strips of land may have been some distance away. This changed with the Enclosure Act of 1768 for Normanton, and many small farmers, who could not afford to fence their strips of land, had to sell them to their wealthier neighbours. As a result the landscape changed in Normanton, as elsewhere: the large open fields were now parcelled out to different owners who planted quickthorn hedges round their plots, and some eventually built themselves farmhouses on their land, thus moving away from the village street.

The agricultural life of Normanton village continued through the years with new names appearing on the scene in the course of time as properties and land changed hands. These include the Goodales, the Radfords of Cottons Farm and Park Hill, John Shaw of Normanton House, members of the Wright family (connected with Butterley Iron Works), and Giles Austin, who built Homelands House and after whom the Austin Estate is named.

There were many gardens and orchards in the village and with its tall elms and chestnut trees it was a charming spot to visit for the townspeople who came over the field paths from Derby.

In Mr Harrison's booklet *The Street Names of Normanton*, he says that the 1865 boundaries of Normanton, which were much more extensive than at present, were as follows: *The northern boundary was the Burton Road — from Warwick Avenue to*

Village Street, looking west, in the early part of this century. Originally known as The Portway, this ancient road ran through Normanton linking east and west.

Breedon Hill Road. An irregular line following the field boundaries was taken to the bottom of Darby Street, thence along Lower Dale Road, Peartree Road and St Thomas's Road to its junction with Balaclava Road. An easterly course was then taken to cross the railway to Elton Road when the southerly course was resumed to include Cottons Farm, and meet the Chellaston Road below Sinfin, returning North to St Stephen's church, then west along Wordsworth Avenue, then south to include the Gudgemoor (Goodsmoor) Farm. Returning northwards to cross Stenson Road at the top of Sunny Hill, when it passed

Another view of Village Street, from the Norman Arms, when small children could stroll unconcernedly down the street, not having to worry about traffic.

down the hill in the rear of the cottages almost to the brook, and then followed the field boundaries to the Burton Road, near Warwick Avenue.

This included the area which became the parish of St Stephen Sinfin, in 1979, and land which is now part of the parishes of St Chad, St Bartholomew, Sinfin Moor, and St Andrew Blagreaves.

Peartree and Normanton railway station was opened on 2 June 1890 with the first train, for Derby, stopping there at 7.41am. Apparently there was a dispute as to who was the first passenger, with Mrs Fanny Brown of 62 Kings Cottages, Harrington Street, claiming precedence over Mrs Mary Brown of Normanton!

In addition to what was to become the familiar landmark of Normanton Barracks on Sinfin Lane (built 1874-1877), more changes were on the way with the continuing industrialisation of Derby. Businessmen and professional people built themselves large houses in Normanton, ancient cottages were demolished and roads widened. Most of the farms disappeared, with the land being used to house the rapidly expanding population (the number of residents in Normanton increased from 638 in 1871 to 3,854 in 1881). The land around the farm where the Sherwood Forester Hotel now stands had houses built on it, and in the 1890s there were building plots for sale fronting Randolph Road, Sackville Street, Chatham Street (or Pelham Street as it was first called) and Village Street. The sale of Colonel Newdigate's estate took place in 1879 and included building land having

a frontage to the new road leading from the Barracks to the village — hence Newdigate Street.

In the 1920s, Derby Corporation bought a large portion of the Cottons Farm and soon houses appeared in Victory Road and the surrounding area. Part of the farm was made into the Municipal Golf Course. The International Combustion Company acquired land for their works, and later another housing estate was developed fronting Sinfin Lane. The industrialisation of Sinfin Lane continued with the Old Brickworks (which had supplied bricks for the building of Normanton Barracks) becoming Richardson's Tannery and the arrival of the Macintosh Cable Company and Hampshire's.

In the early years of this century, Warwick Avenue was being constructed and council houses were being built opposite St Giles' Church, where the Red Thorn Farm once stood. Later on the appearance of the village was altered again with the cutting through of Kenilworth Avenue. In 1878, Derby Corporation had begun to take in parts of Normanton and by 1928 Normanton had become part of the Borough of Derby.

After the death of Mr Austin in 1929, Derby Corporation acquired his land and built the Austin Estate stretching down to Sunny Hill. Normanton House and Homelands House became part of the girls' grammar school, built in 1937 fronting Village Street — originally called Homelands School but now renamed the Village Community School.

The green fields around the village have given way

Showing Sam Walker's cottages in Village Street. Normanton Cottage is in the background.

to streets of houses and it is difficult to imagine the rural atmosphere which still lingers in the memories of some older residents. These lines lamenting the demise of the village were written by Mrs Powell, wife of the village schoolmaster, in the late 1920s.

In days gone by this village of ours
Was shaded and sheltered neath leafy bowers
Its orchards were laden with apple and pear
And sweet-voiced birds built many nests there
'Neath its hawthorn hedges sweet violets grew
In many a sheltered nook we knew
Small cottages faced the village street
Their steps worn hollow by passing feet.
In their gardens gay with old-world flowers
The cottagers spent many pleasant hours.
All round the village were meadows green
And distant hills framed the peaceful scene.
Sweet fragrant scent of new-mown hay
Was borne on the breeze at close of day.
And pathways were green with growing grass
When our grandparents old were lad and lass.
Near by our church gates the red-thorns gay
Delighted our sight for many a day.
And the gnarled pear tree each fair spring time:
Budded and blossomed through shade and shine:
And people came strolling from Derby Town
To see our village in its summer gown.
And probably called on cheese-making day
At the White House Farm for curds and whey.
Where the Sherwood stands was a farmhouse old
With big roomy barns and wide cattle fold
Near by lived a tailor who plied his trade
And on the wayside hedge his goods displayed.
A honey-suckle twined about his door

By the time this photograph was taken, motor vehicles had begun to appear. Here we are looking west, showing cottages near the old school.

And passing sweet were the blooms it bore.
It is said that sportsmen in days of yore
Went hawking with falcons o'er Sinfin Moor.
And that in our midst in days gone by
Lived families old of lineage high.
Though the site of the Hall is covered o'er
The Hall Farm stands with its studded door.
We hear the swish of the scythe no more
Nor the swinging flail on the threshing floor.
Nor the corncrake's call at eventide
Mid the ripening corn where they loved to hide.
No more doth the lark at dawn of day
Lure with its song bright hours away.
Nor building rooks caw in the tall elm trees
Where their nestlings rocked on each passing breeze.
For our village is part of a larger scheme
With a past that is fading like a morning dream.

The Cavendish

AS INDUSTRY came to Derby in the second half of the nineteenth century, the population of Normanton increased considerably. Streets of terraced houses were built to accommodate the employees of the expanding railway workshops and other industries coming into the area around the railway line.

Many were small two or three-bedroomed terraced houses, others more superior villas for higher paid staff and managers. Much of this housing was in the vicinity of the area where five roads meet — Stenson Road, Almond Street, Upper Dale Road, Walbrook Road and Derby Lane. An hotel, the Cavendish, was built on the corner of Upper Dale Road and Walbrook Road in 1898 and gave the area its name. Soon shops sprang to life and the Cavendish became a thriving shopping centre.

In 1910, the Derby Co-operative Provident Society built distinctive premises where Stenson Road joins Almond Street — the Jubilee Hall over the shops presumably being named to commemorate the Diamond Jubilee of the Society. It was 'the most imposing block of branch buildings the Society has ever erected' according to Mr W.Leslie Unsworth in *Seventy-Five Years Co-operation in Derby* published in 1927.

His account goes on: *Here, on a semi-circular frontage, was erected a two-storied building, with shops for grocery, butchery and creamery. The latter department was quite an innovation, but by this time the Society was doing a very considerable milk business, and it was considered advisable to have this Stenson Road branch so designed as to be a branch milk depot for receiving the milk as it was brought in from the farms. All this required ample space, and thus Stenson Road was designed very elaborately, in brick with stone facings. Over the stores was made a hall — one of the best in the town, if not the largest, and, though this district of the town (Normanton) was not then populous, it has grown to considerable dimensions. It was a courageous enterprise at that time . . .the hall at Stenson Road will seat over 400 people comfortably . . .the whole block of premises is not only a credit to the co-operative movement, but to the architecture of the town of Derby itself. Private traders' buildings in the near vicinity are quite dwarfed by this magnificent example of what co-operative enterprise and genius can do.*

The 'private traders' included Bradley's men's wear next door, along with Lewis' Drapery, the Meadow Dairy and Peters' greengrocery shop which was on the corner of Vincent Street. On the opposite corner was Miller's sweet shop 'Le Bon Chocolat' next to Watson's the chemists, with further on the Cosmea seed shop, 'Arlene' the hairdresser, and a butcher's shop.

The bottom of Derby Lane boasted Mr G.F.Dyer's music shop, Edwards' fruit shop and the Post Office, with Ingle's garage, Oakley's hardware shop and Dorothy Selby, hairdresser, around the corner in Walbrook Road.

The Derby Pavilion pictured in 1920. The site later became the Cavendish Cinema and later a supermarket.

A gentlemen, minding the baby, raises his hat to a group of ladies in Normanton Park in the golden days before World War One.

COUNTY BOROUGH OF DERBY.

NORMANTON RECREATION GROUND.

OPENED BY

HIS GRACE THE DUKE OF DEVONSHIRE.

CORNELIUS BOAM, SEPTEMBER 4TH 1909. W. BLEWS ROBOTHAM
CHAIRMAN. MAYOR

Commemorative stone plaque marking the opening of Normanton Park.

In the triangle formed by the junction of Upper Dale Road and Almond Street was the bakery and shop of Birds the Confectioners, (where Peach's bakery was previously), the delicious aroma floating from the bakehouse ensuring that the shop was never short of customers, and the warmth of the bakery wall on Upper Dale Road providing a comfortable leaning place for passengers waiting for the tramcars on cold winter mornings. Here also was the Tramways Department clock with the box where conductors 'checked in' on the route back into town.

The Cavendish was not only known for its shops — entertainment came to Normanton as early as 1902 when a local farmer allowed the erection of a marquee on one of his fields at the junction of Stenson Road and Derby Lane. This was used for auctions and local talent competitions at first, but by 1910 a music licence had been granted and touring concert parties and

This building, pictured in February 1992, formerly housed a café. It is situated near the Cavendish entrance to Normanton Park.

repertory companies were delighting the audiences there. Some of these performers were to achieve national acclaim in later years.

The original marquee was replaced by a more substantial wooden structure, with accommodation for between 600 and 800 people, with the 'chicken run' at the back of the hall providing standing room for the youngsters of the day at 3d a time.

By the beginning of World War One, the Derby Pierrot Pavilion, as it was then called, was a popular rendezvous for Derbeians: those not within walking distance could take the tramcar from the town or the Midland Railway Station to the Cavendish. Performances continued throughout the war years, local talent also having an opportunity to appear there. It was a comfortable place, warm in winter and cool in summer when the side panels were opened to let in the air. For many people it was a regular weekly venue — a place to meet friends — and after the show many a romance blossomed as the smartly-dressed young men and women met in groups or paraded to and fro on the pavement between the Co-op shops and the gates of Normanton Park.

Sadly, the Pavilion met with disaster in early January 1929 when it was destroyed by fire. It was not rebuilt, and for a while there was a pitch and putt golf course on the site. It was not until 1937 that it was replaced by the new Cavendish Cinema built by local businessmen at a cost of £30,000. On 31 December 1937 the *Derbyshire Advertiser* reported that the opening ceremony and showing of the first film, *For You Alone* starring Grace Moore, was attended by the Mayor, Alderman E.Paulson, and members of the Town Council. A handsome souvenir programme in a silver cover was produced for the opening with an introduction which said: *The modern cinema has become a necessity in the lives of people. After the toil of the day, it has become necessary to relax, to be entertained — to be interested in something different — and one could not enjoy the relaxation more than in a luxury cinema such as the Cavendish, which will fill a long-felt want in the Normanton district.*

Mr Bryce Hanmer, on behalf of the directors, said every endeavour would be made to give patrons the films they wanted, but the problem of obtaining films was more difficult than people imagined! However, the cinema carried on, surviving World War Two, until it was closed down in 1960 by the then owners, the Rank Organisation, and subsequently demolished to the regret of many local people.

The site was taken over by a subsidiary company for development as a supermarket which was opened in 1965 by Fine Fare (now Gateway). It was reported to be the first British supermarket which had a drive-in car park at the front!

The Derby Co-operative store at the Cavendish pictured between the wars.

In the years that followed changes to the other shops at the Cavendish took place. The Co-op closed its shops and others changed hands. When Birds moved their shop to Walbrook Road and built a new bakery at Ascot Drive, the old buildings were pulled down and the corner site is now occupied by a garage and petrol station.

The changes are obvious to those who have known the area for many years and although it does not appear as attractive as it was earlier in the century, it is still a busy shopping centre for the local community. A large traffic island has been installed to ease the heavy traffic flow and, for most of the year, its flowers provide a splash of colour to enliven the scene.

Normanton Recreation Ground was developed on the site of old brick yards and opened by the Duke of Devonshire on 4 September 1909. *The Derby Mercury* for 3 September 1909 informed its readers that: *'There will be a garden party from three to five for which convenient arrangements have been made for a three-minute service of trams from the Royal on the circular route. The Duke of Devonshire will motor from Chatsworth and will arrive at the ground about five and the opening ceremony to which the general public will be admitted will commence at 5.30, the Mayor presiding. The Bishop of Southwell will offer the dedicatory prayers and the Mayor will make a few opening remarks and will present His Grace with a golden key and ask him to declare the ground open.*

The Duke will deliver the address and drive round the ground opening the Chatsworth Street and Fairfield Road entrance. Sir Thomas Roe, MP, will move and Sir Henry Bemrose second, a vote of thanks to His Grace . . .The following bands will play in different parts of the ground: 5th Battalion Sherwood Foresters, Derby Sax Tuba and Derby Excelsior. In a tent near the centre of the ground the celebrated "Brownies" Musical Society Entertainers will perform and on another platform Professor Carl will conjure and the Minster Glee Singers and Miss Norah Jervis sing. 30 gentlemen will kindly act as stewards. The bands and entertainers will play and perform until dusk.'

Its extent of approximately 30 acres contained tennis courts, bowling green and two children's playgrounds — one for boys and one for girls — with plenty of space for football, cricket and a bandstand. The iron gates at the entrances were locked at night after the bell had rung. The children's playgrounds were surrounded by iron railings and woe betide any child who invaded the playground of the opposite sex! The park keepers kept constant watch, picking up litter on their spiked sticks as they patrolled.

There have been extensions and modifications over the years and the Recreation Ground is now known as Normanton Park. Many of the iron railings were removed during World War Two and one of Derby's barrage balloons and a static water tank were sited on the football field. The World War One tank which had been on display at the corner opposite the main

The Cavendish looking towards the Cavendish Hotel public house and Bird's Bakery. A tram is coming up Walbrook Road.

gates also disappeared and in the affluent 1960s, Derby Parks Department enlivened this spot with many delightful flower beds, also alongside Stenson Road, until shortage of funds curtailed their activities.

The swings, seesaws, slides and climbing bars in the playgrounds deteriorated and were replaced by an open unisex play area with modern equipment and a mountain of earth for intrepid climbers. A new pavilion, changing-rooms and recreation rooms have been built and a car park provided at the corner of Warwick Avenue and Colwyn Avenue and the entrances, now five, are permanently open. There are not so many tennis courts as there were originally and two hard courts have been adapted for other games with floodlighting, but Normanton Park remains a popular place for recreation and leisure for young and old.

Before 1922 there was no road alongside the Recreation Ground beyond Stenson Road until Warwick Avenue was constructed to become one of the sections of Derby's ring-road. This was followed in the 1930s by the opening of Kenilworth Avenue from the junction of Warwick Avenue and Stenson Road, cutting across Derby Lane to Village Street and Newdigate Street. Housing developed rapidly, with side roads joining this new section of ring road to the old village.

Although by the beginning of the war in 1939, Normanton had lost its fields, considerable areas of allotment gardens had been laid out and some still exist along the south side of Warwick Avenue and the east boundary of the Park. However, the extensive area to the south of the Junior School, down the old 'cinder path', has been swallowed up by post-war housing and nearly all the allotments on the west side of Stenson Road have been built over in recent years.

Normanton Barracks

IT MUST have caused a stir in the little village of Normanton when the building of Normanton Barracks began in 1874, and again when it opened in 1877 as HQ No 26 Brigade Depot for the 54th and 95th Regiments.

When one of the first contingents of the 54th and 95th Regiments arrived at Derby Station on 1 December 1877, on their way to the newly-erected barracks, they were met by the Mayor of Derby and members of the Corporation and then marched to Normanton Barracks led by the bands of the Militia and Volunteers.

That there had been some apprehension in Normanton about the coming of the military is evident from Mr John Shaw's remarks in 1881. He is reported as saying that although they were very much afraid when they heard that these soldiers were coming amongst them, they all now felt great respect for the officers and men who had lived amongst them since the establishment of the depot.

As a result of Lord Cardwell's Army reorganisation, the 45th (Nottinghamshire Regiment), the Nottinghamshire Militia, the 95th (Derbyshire Regiment) and the Derbyshire Militia came together to form The Sherwood Foresters in 1881. The HQ of the regiment and its depot occupied the barracks under the title 'HG 45th Regimental District'.

The barracks became very much a part of Norman-ton. St Giles was the garrison church, with the vicar as their chaplain. Church parade on Sunday mornings drew many spectators as the soldiers, dressed in red coats in the early days, marched from the barracks to the church led by the band and their regimental mascot, the ram. The history of the mascot goes back to the time in 1838 when the regiment was sailing from Ireland to Ceylon and a local raja came aboard and gave the regiment a ram. Presented continuously since 1858: he is known as Private Derby and is officially on the strength! Replacements came from the Duke of Devonshire's flock at Chatsworth.

The men always sat in the south aisle of St Giles' Church and it became known as the 'soldier aisle'. Their Colours laid up in the church were a familiar sight for many years but have been removed to the regimental museum at Nottingham Castle for preservation.

Every year on Badajoz Day, 6 April, a red tunic was flown from the flagpole at the barracks. This commemorated the action during the Peninsular War in Spain (1808-1814) at the Battle of Badajoz when a detachment of the 45th Regiment managed to get into the castle, and the red coat of one of the officers was hoisted on the flagpole in place of the French flag to indicate the capture of the castle. A red tunic is still flown from Derby Council House on 6 April each year.

Officers' Mess and Quarters.

Chatsworth Block and Marabout Block.

Normanton Barracks Square, where thousands of servicemen received their basic training.

The annual pilgrimage to Crich Memorial commemorating the men from the regiment who died in two world wars takes place on the first Sunday in July, following a service at St Giles' Church.

The depot mobilised in 1899 for the Boer War and an intensive period began as regulars, militia and volunteers passed on their way to and from South Africa. August 1914 saw intensive activity again. The 3rd Reserve (Militia) were mobilised in the depot and many hundreds of regimental reservists passed through on their way to the regular battalions. On 9 August 1914, the volunteers for 'Kitchener's Army' began to come in and by 15 August, 5,000 men were at Normanton Barracks to form the 9th, 10th, 11th and 12th Sherwood Foresters Battalions. Throughout World War One, a constant stream of men passed through the Barracks, including recruits to training battalions and wounded men coming back from hospitals. It was the centre of activity for a great regiment of 33 battalions training or fighting throughout the world.

When the depot started mobilising the regiment

The Armoury at Normanton Barracks.

Normanton Barracks, opened in 1877, looks sad and neglected when this photograph of the main gate was taken in 1980. The Barracks were demolished two years later.

for World War Two, the training centre expanded and took over Markeaton Hall, Allestree Hall and Egginton Hall. The regiment expanded to 15 battalions. The actual barracks became accommodation for Army personnel connected with the Ordnance Depot in Sinfin Lane.

In 1946, the barracks once more returned to its normal role of Regimental HQ and recruit training depot of the Sherwood Foresters. However, as a result of cuts in the Army's strength and reorganisation of the methods of training recruits, the last Foresters left Normanton Barracks in 1963. In February 1970, the Sherwood Foresters Regiment amalgamated with the Worcestershire Regiment and became the Worcestershire & Sherwood Foresters Regiment.

Growing on the far side of the barrack square near the sports field, was an historical tree, the 'Napoleon Willow'. A cutting was taken from the willow

New recruits enjoy a spot of relaxation after arriving at Normanton Barracks in July 1939, as war clouds gathered over Europe.

Edwardian Derbeians listen to the band at Normanton Barracks in 1904.

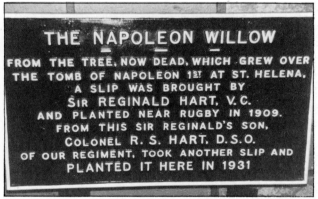

This plaque, which once marked a famous local tree, is now in Derby Museum.

growing over Napoleon's grave on St Helena in 1909 and planted in Rugby, and in 1932 a cutting from this tree was planted at Normanton Barracks. After the barracks was demolished in 1982, cuttings were taken from the tree in the hope that one would eventually be planted at the new development to be known as Foresters Park. Although this has not yet happened, one of the cuttings is still in the care of Derby City Council Leisure Services Department.

At the Territorial Army Centre in Sinfin Lane there is a large willow tree which was grown from a cutting from the tree at Normanton Barracks, and the main gates from the entrance to the barracks have also been

installed there.

The original plaque about the Napoleon Willow is now in Derby Museum. Also on display is a revolving sentry box from Normanton Barracks, with a model of a soldier in the uniform of the Sherwood Foresters Notts & Derby Regiment of 1913 vintage.

What greater contrast could there be than the redeveloped barracks site which includes in its facilities a multi-screen cinema, an hotel and restaurant, tenpin bowling and a bingo hall . . .Only the name, the Forester Leisure Park, contains a reminder of the old familiar Normanton Barracks.

Some Reminiscences

Memories of Village Life

Mrs Claudia Flinn

VILLAGE Street, I can just recall before it was widened and the housing on the north side commenced. I was born in Balaclava Road in 1916, at a time when the only houses beyond Normanton Barracks were the railway cottages on the Sinfin Lane Bridge. Before the widening of Newdigate Street there was a large field on the south side, surrounded by a hawthorn hedge.

We children must have used a gap in this to gain entrance, as I never remember a gate, but this field furnished us with all the flowers we needed for our daisy and buttercup chains for May and Empire Days. Near its junction with Village Street, there was a group of trees (a few still remain), and a large hollow which we called Dingley Dell and which was a good playground. At the opposite end, facing the barracks, was a clay bank, steeper at one end than the other. Timid children who daren't keep on their feet to run down this, slithered down, with dire results to lace-trimmed knickers!

Another playground, although not strictly in Old Normanton, was Calvary Brook, that ran from the Sunnyhill allotments across the fields, to the golf course on Sinfin Lane. In this brook, the girls paddled and found violets on the banks, the boys armed with fishing nets and jam-jars, caught minnows, which sadly, never seemed to live long on the kitchen window sill.

As we went to Pear Tree School, we knew little of the Normanton Day School, but the church, and Sunday school, figured quite a lot in our young lives. Attendance on Sunday afternoons at the latter was a 'must' until school-leaving age. Winter evenings, I sometimes went to church with my mother, and remember the warm, comfortable atmosphere when the lights were lowered during the sermons. I always went to sleep.

At this time I remember well Giles Austin, and Captain Bennett, who read the lessons. He lived in Village Street, towards the Norman Arms and played such a big part in the 4th Derwent Scout Group. At this time Mr Price was the vicar, with Mr Roberts, his curate. Mr Price had an imposing wife, who was rather awe-inspiring to us youngsters, as she swept into church with her two daughters, just before the announcing of the first hymn.

One of these daughters married the son of Mr Grimes, a Derby business man, who lived at Park Hill. The son was a naval officer, and it was a very pretty wedding, with an accent on white fur capes, and muffs to match, the latter decorated with artificial holly.

Cottage attached to the back of Barley Row, opposite Old Normanton Post Office.

Occupants of a cottage opposite Old Normanton Post Office.

Village Street looking west from the entrance to Normanton Cottage.

Church activities in the Old School Hall, included GFS (Girls' Friendly Society) on Mondays and YPU (Young Persons' Union) on Wednesdays. We went to the latter, though I'm not quite sure what were its aims, except that we did have occasional magic lantern slides of a missionary nature — David Livingstone and Mary Slessor. I'm sure also, we made nuisances of ourselves, outside, daring each other to approach near to Lake House, which was said to be 'haunted'. I have no recollection of adults accompanying children, even on winter evenings. Big sisters looked after little ones, and we all went home together. The only instruction I ever heard to the bigger girls was that they 'keep away from those barracks gates!' Of course, traffic was very light in those days, even after dark.

We took very much for granted the presence of the soldiers, bugle calls and church parades. One of my very first memories was being wakened up in the night by a loud rumbling in the street. I was told afterwards it was a tank going up to the Barracks after returning from the Great War. I wonder whether this was the one that stood in Normanton Recreation Ground for years.

On summer Sunday evenings our family of six walked through and round the parish. One walk was up Cabbage Square, down the cinder path, roughly the present Coleridge Street, across to the Old Devil's Bridge over the railway, and up Sinfin Lane, home. This was before Macintosh Cables (afterwards the Ordnance Factory) and Hampshire's were built, and certainly no housing estates were there.

I did not know that St Giles' Hall and the Old School Hall no longer belonged to the church. For the building of the former, we children were encouraged to contribute one penny a brick.

Mrs Cooper was well-known to us, and for years our Christmas Day breakfast was a Cooper's pork pie.

Normanton Barracks
Mr W.Pegg, Village Street

THE barracks used Old Normanton Post Office. Four soldiers with rifles went to fetch the mail night and morning, taking with them a man in 'jankers' to carry it. The *Last Post* sounded at 10pm and people in the village timed their watches by it.

From Derby Evening Telegraph
'Bygones'

. . .THE top of Browning Street was known locally as Cabbage Square.

Opposite Mr Giles Austin's house was a house where the Grimes family lived. They owned a drapers' shop on The Spot, where you would always get most polite service.

There was a large orchard and five small cottages on one side of the road, where modern bungalows are now. On the corner of Village Street was Cooper's

Old cottages in Village Street, pictured in 1913, where the war memorial now stands. Mr Booth's farm is on the left.

sweet shop and bakery — the smell from the new bread was delicious.

Along Derby Lane, standing a little way back, was a house that looked derelict and empty. It was reputed to be haunted, and we always scuttled past.

Where the Austin Estate is now was just a field of buttercups, with a cinder path down one side and allotments on the other.

Memories of Old Normanton
Mrs Kathleen Beeston (neé Baker)
I REMEMBER many old cottages — for this was really a separate village, not part of Derby — farms and farmworkers' cottages, gentlemen's houses in their own grounds. Some of the cottages had real country gardens growing their own vegetables and flowers, and I remember one that grew herbs for medicinal purposes, threepence a bottle for 'Cough Stuff' (very good), no National Health, and doctors cost money, but you must take your own bottle. I once made the dreadful mistake of going without a bottle and was asked, "What are you going to put it in, your pocket?" So far as I remember, all the medicines were liquid.

The Barracks
What a difference the Sunday Church Parade made. I remember the beautiful bright uniforms (before khaki came in), the instruments gleaming in the sun and the sound of the band coming along the lane to church. One aisle was reserved for the soldiers. Officers and wives (and children) sat apart, and they *could* sing. A great addition to the ordinary congregation.

Homelands
Mr Giles Austin built this lovely modern house for his family, with beautiful green lawns and gardens. Mr Austin was churchwarden and always came to church carrying a black leather bag, which I presume was for taking home the church collections. His daughter, Miss Gertrude, had a great influence on the young girls in the village. She took a Bible class on Sundays, remembering girls' birthdays, and other activities for them in the week in connection with missionary work.

Mr Austin gave to the church a field down Sunny Hill for the purpose of sporting activities, for the use of the churchgoers. We girls and young women started to learn how to play cricket. We had to know the rules, attend practice, and we wore a uniform. There were tennis courts, football areas and playing places for children, with a wooden hut as changing room. The visiting teams were entertained to tea afterwards in the Old School in Village Street. In the winter we played hockey and football with equal enjoyment.

Reminiscences of St Giles' Hockey Club and Ladies' Cricket team
Miss Dorothy I.Elliott
AFTER the holocaust of the First World War, young men and women were catered for by Normanton St Giles' church. A sports field was provided adjacent to Stenson Road and bounded by Cuttle Brook. Football, cricket, hockey and tennis clubs were formed.

Before joining the hockey club, I served an apprenticeship as lineswoman and washer-up in the schoolroom after giving tea to a visiting team. This gave me time to acquire a six-pleated tunic of sandy-brown distinguished by two braids of red and green, a hockey stick, pads and boots.

We were honoured to have with us the doctor's wife, Mrs Patey, curate's wife Mrs Roberts and Miss G.Austin, younger daughter of Mr Giles Austin. We learnt much from members who were teachers —

Barley Row, Normanton.

St Giles' Ladies Hockey Club, pictured in the 1920s.

Frances and Dorothy Holmes. Elizabeth Clifton, Clarrie Buckle, Mary Salt and the two referees Mr Basford and Councillor Wilkinson. Louie Rimmington was the honorary secretary.

Our 'away' matches necessitated walking or cycling to Borrowash, Rose Hill, Parkfields Cedars, the (then) Deaf and Dumb School, Sawley and Melbourne: Mr Salt's bus took us to Belper, Chesterfield, Cromford and Ambergate, but for Shottle, Idridgehay, Turnditch and Wirksworth we travelled by train at a cheaper rate, twelve for the price of eleven. It was said on the Wirksworth line, "You could sow seeds on the outward journey and gather flowers on the return!"

The club's enthusiasm earned them a mention in the local paper.

The cricket team included Bessie Baker, the stonewaller of our team. Elsie Glover, the grass-cutting bowler. Gladys Glover and my sister, Flossie, the good runners, Winnie Wibberley the wicket-keeper, and the two over-arm bowlers, Mary Hammond and Doris Walker, on whom the team relied. They wore trousers and rode a motor bike! The secretary was Louie Rimmington.

The original Norman Arms, Village Street.

I'll never forget playing against Duffield at the Eyes Meadow, for we walked all the way from Derby and back. We must have been tired before we started. Doris and Mary, who came by the motor bike, scored the only runs. We were all out for six!

An Octogenarian's Recollections of the Cavendish Area c.1911-1970

Miss Doris Lester

I DO not remember moving to Cameron Road when I was around three years old. A clear memory which must have been around 1912 is of going to the 'Rec' (Normanton Recreation Ground) with my mother and a neighbour to, presumably, school sports. It is just a memory of crowds of parents, seated on benches set in a large circle on the large area next to where the tennis courts are now situated. Later I recall going to play on the 'Rec' in the play area set aside for girls.

In this area was, I believe, a single-deck old tram-car which was a great attraction. The swings, roundabout and the 'ladders' . . .these were set at an angle starting around a child's height and slanting upwards until nearly twice the height, and children, myself amongst them, worked their way hand over hand on the rungs of the ladder to the centre and down the other side. I recall my reward for great enthusiasm was very painful blisters on both hands.

The Corporation houses near the Cavendish and Derby Lane area were not built until after the First War . . .and we reached the Cavendish. *ie* as far as the hotel, by walking across the 'Top Greens', en route to the Rec or the Co-op shops which, as far as I recall, were about the only shops there except for Lewis' Drapery, a stationers & toy shop, where the fish and chip shop now is — and the shop on

the corner, although on the other side of Vincent Street, the corner shop was 'Le Bon Chocolat' and Watson's the chemist next door.

There were no Corporation houses at that time and I still recall the thrill of seeing a wee brown fieldmouse scoot into the hedges as I passed.

The 'outdoor' department of the Cavendish Hotel was where the brick entrance porch is at present, but in my childhood the entrance was up a few stone steps with very open iron rails. Don't remember seeing any boys doing as some girls did: that was, passing both the bottom left and right of your coat over the top rail — and swinging in the space between the rail and the floor. I never tore my coat!

The Co-op distributed milk from a large depot at the side of the grocery store. The grocery and provisions shop seemed very big — lots of space between the 'dry' goods — the bacon, butter and other products. Customers went to one counter and if, say, the majority of items were bought there — and just one other item needed from the other side of the shop, the assistant would call out in a loud voice, "Two pounds of sugar paid for please". And the shopper nipped over and picked it up.

The assistant's reckoning fascinated me, for if a few items were involved, the assistant would put a hand over each item as he (and I think it was always 'he') added up — like two and two — three and six — then whilst calculating the next item would say 'three and six — four and eleven — four and eleven — six and five — and so on. Then he would make out the check (in triplicate I think). Later, it was interesting when they installed a cash desk — and sent the metal containers thereto — with the check and cash inside — and back came any change.

The manager of the grocery department was a Mr

Hallsworth's Bakery at the top of Derby Lane. Further on, council houses opposite St Giles' Church are being built.

Garrett — a very nice gentlemanly figure — and when children may be misbehaving or just being a nuisance to customers and staff, Mr Garrett would shout, 'Now children — recreation ground farther up the road . . .'' The butcher's shop was not of great interest to me — I'm no good at choosing meat, even now! But I'm sure good service was always given by the manager and his assistants. The then dairy — I really liked that shop — was where I was sometimes sent for an 'Elf Loaf'. At least that is what I asked for but was given the 'Health Loaf', a currant loaf for the small sum of sixpence.

The Pavilion was a very popular 'theatre' — that is a courtesy title. Usually revues were put on for the entertainment of audiences. Many will remember Fred Terry and his wife, who spent many weeks there each year — and with a cast of only about six put on quite good little shows. A pleasant feature was the fact it was kept lovely and cool in the hot weather — as the wooden partitions (instead of glass windows) could be taken out. Many locals went each week to the Pavilion — indeed, half the audience had received free tickets!

I could not leave 'Walter' out of this recollection for he really was a feature. The 'Company' composed a song about him but, sadly, I do not remember it. I do not remember when the Pavilion was burnt down but it must have been after 1926 — then for some years it created interest as a miniature golf — or was it a golf-putting course — which sounds a bit grand . . .The Cavendish Cinema followed the golf — and I'm sure it was very popular, but sadly no doubt with

the increasing interest in television, the cinema was demolished and made way for the first supermarket there — I forget which one it was, but it did not do the Co-op much good.

The Cavendish, too, was a popular area for young people and many friendships betwixt young men and maidens were forged. My older brother was wont to tease my elder sister about the 'Monkey Run', and I have seen among my sister's treasures a photograph of a number of young men taken on a camping holiday, with the caption 'Cav Pals'.

Whit Tuesday afternoons were of interest. All the Sunday Schools in that area congregated for a service on the Rec to Bands, and led by pupils upholding their Sunday School banner for the combined service. At the Jubilee Hall, I think the 'Penny Bank' staff visited on Friday evenings, when children took small sums to save. The hall could be engaged for concerts, meetings, weddings, and there was a regular weekly dance. A pleasant light room with a good dance floor.

No doubt there are other writings on the subject of the Sherwood Foresters church parade, but it seemed to me as a child that swarms of people went up Derby Lane on Sunday mornings, particularly when it was known the ram mascot and a band would lead the parade.

At the PSA at Duncan Road Temperance Hall, musical afternoons were held. In the spring or summer of 1919, an effort was made, I think probably through day schools, to ensure that all children were enrolled in a Sunday School, thereby ensuring they were able to take part in a special parade and tea-party, similar

Looking east along Village Street. Note the splendid Chestnut tree.

to Whitsuntide treats, to commemorate the end of the war. I recall the huge procession on that day, being part of it. Interesting, too, on these treat days, was the appearance of the cart-horses, loaned by the Co-op coal department and maybe Offiler's Brewery, the horses and drays being colourfully decorated with ribbons etc., by the drivers, the young children being carried on the decorated drays.

Extracts from *A Vicarage Childhood*
Dorothy Jeffery (neé Bull)

WE raced up and down the lawn, playing hockey with croquet mallets, and we shouted through treacle-tin and string telephones, our excited voices conveying messages from one end of the garden to the other. We zoomed down the drive in an old pram, our progress on to the road stopped only by the closed gate. Twenty times around the house we rode, covering a mile, our bicycle wheels scattering the gravel and churning up the paths. Our brother's tent, pitched on the front lawn near the cedar tree was our camp, palace, stable, fortress or garage, according to the requirements of our games. Our tricycle was in turn a fiery steed pounding the turf, or a noisy motor bike, etching tyre marks into the smooth green turf.

Inside, the vicarage provided many opportunities for our imaginations to be expressed in lively and dangerous games. Down the stairs we hurtled on a tin tray. We scrambled in and out of the arch-shaped bannisters. Around the kitchen we pranced, bearing flaming torches kindled at the kitchen stove. This was known as 'The Ancient Briton Game.' Obviously such activities were fraught with danger, but I think we were blissfully unaware of the possible consequences. Another noisy activity we enjoyed was 'The

William the Conqueror Game' which involved leaping from the back of the sofa, and jumping from chair to chair, bouncing on their sagging springs. Of course, such activities were not encouraged by our parents, but my sister and I were very good at protesting our innocence and quickly restoring order!

We delighted in dressing up and acting plays for whoever would watch our "entertainment" and we revelled in dancing to the music provided by an old collection of operatic records on an ancient wind-up gramophone given to us by a parishioner.

Schools and hospitals were improvised for our dolls, and our brother built villages of mud huts in the garden. Such activities were prophetic: my sister became a nurse, I became a teacher, and our brother spent several years in Africa as an official in the Colonial Service.

It was a delight and a privilege to be a vicarage child. Our years at Normanton Vicarage have left lasting and happy memories of a childhood enriched by the affectionate interest of many kind people. We remember happy times spent with parishioners, and still enjoy friendships begun during those years.

Extract from the *Derby Evening Telegraph* 26 September 1945, from a letter by Mrs E.Powell, wife of the village schoolmaster. She died in 1949, aged 92.

. . .WE publish a letter from an 88-year-old lady who, being bedridden with arthritis, has to write lying on her back:

"I have many and varied recollections of the once interesting and rural village of Normanton.

"Although . . .there was no village green there, at the crossroads there was the pinfold, and besides the various farms there were groups of old-world

Village Street pictured when it was safe to stroll along the road, or even pause to chat.

cottages, many with stone steps worn hollow by footsteps of long-forgotten dwellers in the quaint homesteads.

"One tiny cottage was occupied by a tailor, who made boys' clothing and displayed his goods on a nearby hedge. This cottage was in the centre of the village.

"In the grounds of Lake House, which I heard was once a farmhouse, there was a large barn built of bricks. This barn's gable end faced Derby Lane and the date 1716 was outlined in blue bricks. It was mostly passed by, unnoticed, for the date was seldom mentioned, and time had weathered the brickwork.

"I have often wondered if some ancient hall may have been in this village, as there are blocks of stone here and there. You may see these old stones on the right hand side of Vicarage Lane (now Browning Street). They form the foundation of a barn near a few cottages.

"Where the Sherwood Hotel now stands was a rambling farmhouse. Over the gable end was a small window over which was a stone slab, and carved on it were the words 'Cheese Room'. Where streets now run were pastures and allotment gardens, and on the opposite side an apple orchard.

Christmas Joints

"The squire and his wife practically ruled the village. They occupied Normanton House. The wife was head of the Sunday School, and provided the treats and prizes, and they both were keenly interested in the domestic affairs of each parishioner.

"The children's treats were held in a meadow adjoining their house, and at Christmas every parishioner was provided with a joint for the Christmas dinner. A dray covered by a white cloth went round delivering the joints — from a beast fed on the nearby pasture land.

"There were several wells for public use, with windlass and bucket. From the top of Vicarage Lane a wide and extensive view was visible, and I heard that from a specially selected site, the crucifix in Charnwood Forest might be seen. Breedon Church was clearly visible. Now the village is a huddled mass of streets and buildings, and all trace of the country scene has vanished.

Wayside Violets

"When I first knew Derby Lane, tall hawthorn hedges bordered the wayside, and I have actually gathered violets near their roots. A very old lady told me that once a brook trickled down this lane, which was then called Dyke Lane. Does this account for Walbrook Road?

"I have also heard that in far-off days hawking was common on Sinfin Moor, so I suppose falcolnry was then a pastime and custom.

"In the centre of the village was the village pub, a place where the affairs of the nation were fully discussed and settled to the satisfaction of all concerned. How unassuming, comfortable and cosy this hostel was, clean and cool in summer, warm and cosy in the winter.

"At the back was a meadow, with seats provided for those who wished to spend an evening in the open air or have a friendly game of skittles on the nearby alley. This once-humble wayside inn is now an ambitious-looking imitation of a modern town hotel.

Fading Customs

"At the opposite end of the village is the Grange Hotel. At one time this was a sedate, secluded private house, with a long tree-shaded carriage drive.

"And so changes come, and gradually our old-time buildings, people and customs fade. As time rolls on they are forgotten and looked upon as crude and unworthy relics of a past age, but they were anything but that, many of these aged men were expert agriculturists and clever craftsmen: their knowledge gained in the school of experience; able and capable of tackling many problems, which helped to make their and our lives happy, interesting and contented."

John Shaw junior, pictured outside Normanton House.

St Giles' Clergymen

The Revd J.H.Lester, the first Vicar of Normanton after it became a separate parish in 1877, was an outstanding man and evidently one who got things done. An extract from Mr Joe Harrison's *History of Normanton-by-Derby and its Church* quotes a report on what had been accomplished by Mr Lester in two and a half years of ministry at Normanton, and gives a vivid picture of the intense activity in the parish due to his zeal:

"Prior to his coming, the church was almost deserted, there were neither day nor Sunday schools, no vicarage, no endowment, and all fees had to be paid to St Peter's. Now all was changed, the church was filled, there were many regular communicants, day and Sunday schools were established, the disused old chapel being converted into a schoolroom, a moderate endowment for the church had been provided, a site purchased for a vicarage and funds to build this were being earnestly sought. Mr Lester was well-known as a mission preacher, having worked with the Revd W.H.M.H.Aitken. The previous winter he had held five 'twelve-day Missions' in various large towns for which he had received a grant from the Aitken Memorial Fund which enabled him to have the assistance of a curate . . ."

The Revd J.H.Walmsley came to Normanton in 1898. He was a bachelor and remained so. His mother and two sisters lived with him at the Vicarage, his father having died a few years previously. He was a well-loved man, regarded as a friend by parishioners. However, he was said to be a trifle disorganised as he had a habit of appearing just in the nick of time for services and engagements. This did not unduly worry his congregation as they knew he would arrive eventually! People were used to seeing him tearing about on his bicycle and children playing on the streets learned to hop out of his way. In addition to his parish work, Mr Walmsley was Chaplain to the Barracks and to the Derby Workhouse: he also spoke frequently at the breakfast-hour services at the Midland Railway. The major extension to the church took place during his time.

Mr Walmsley was made Bishop of Sierra Leone in 1910 and died in Freetown in 1922 — 'the best-loved man on the West Coast, bar none' (from *John Walmsley. A memoir for his Friends* by E.G.Walmsley.)

In 1920 **The Revd Robert Price** was appointed Vicar of Normanton. He was Irish and spoke with a strong

The Revd Robert Price is talking to Mrs Slater at the Mothers' Union garden party.

Irish brogue that was sometimes difficult to understand! However, he was held in very great affection in the parish and a carved wooden screen to his memory was erected in the chancel in 1947. It was placed in its present position in front of the gallery in 1973. St Giles' Hall was built in Mr Price's time on land given by Mr Giles Austin at the corner of Underhill Avenue and Village Street.

Following the building of the new housing estate at Sinfin and the consequent increase in population, Mr Price put forward the idea of the provision of a church for that area, which resulted in the building of St Stephen's Church at Sinfin. This became a parish in its own right in 1979.

The Revd George McAlpine's ministry, which began in 1936, saw the start of World War Two. He suffered the tragedy of losing his only son in that conflict.

The Revd Kenneth Skelton came to St Giles' Church in 1941 to start his first curacy and later married a

The Rt Revd Kenneth Skelton, a former curate at St Giles' who later became Bishop of Matabeleland, he was also the Bishop of Lichfield, 1975-1984. A British Prime Minister described him as 'courageous'.

Normanton girl, Miss Phyllis Emerton. He was Bishop of Matabeleland (Western Rhodesia and Botswana) from 1962-1970, being there in the difficult days after Rhodesia declared independence. Because of his stance against racialist policies, he was twice named in the Rhodesian parliament as a Communist

and was closely watched by the police. Sir Harold Wilson refers to him in one of his books as 'the courageous Bishop Skelton'. He was appointed Bishop of Lichfield in 1975. Since his retirement in 1984, he has been an Honorary Assistant Bishop in the Derby Diocese.

The Revd Ben Bull who was appointed in 1943, was also a wartime incumbent. He was very much involved with the Forces' Club at St Giles' Hall and Padre's Hour for the many members of the Forces stationed in the parish. Mr Bull is remembered for his warm genial manner, and during his time the Thanksgiving for Victory Memorial window in the east end of the church was installed.

The Revd George Stevens, who came to Normanton as Vicar 1949, was appointed Rural Dean of Derby during his time here. He had a particular interest in the church's Ministry amongst Jews. As well as being a frequent leader of groups on visits to the Holy Land, he published books about Jewish customs and their Christian relevance. He was a gifted preacher and his sermons were a well-known feature of his ministry.

The Revd George Seamer appointed in 1957 was a notable evangelical clergyman who exercised a powerful preaching ministry, and there were changes in church life at St Giles' during his incumbency. The Annual Seamer Memorial Sermon undertaken by well-known evangelical preachers has been held at St Giles' Church since Mr Seamer's death in 1971.

The Revd Canon Barrie Blowers has the distinction of being the longest-serving incumbent of St Giles' Church since Normanton-by-Derby became a separate benefice (1877), being in office from 1969 until his retirement in July 1993.

He was Rural Dean of Derby from 1974-1979, and when the Derby Deanery was split into Derby North and Derby South he became Rural Dean of Derby South from 1979-1989. He was made an Honorary Canon of Derby Cathedral in 1985 and appointed Canon Emeritus upon his retirement. Canon Blowers is held in high regard and his caring ministry has earned him a place in the affections of the people of Normanton.

Tangible reminders of his time in office are the replacement of the two older church halls with a modern church centre, the acquisition of a modern house for the curate, and the building of a new vicarage.

As a licensed Reader, Mrs Blowers was the first clergy wife in Normanton to hold that qualification, and her ministry was valued both at St Giles' and in other churches where she took services from time to time.

Canon Blowers' interest in the history of St Giles' Church prompted him to suggest the Normanton Local History Festival, which took place in May 1992. The Festival revealed a keen interest in Normanton, not only by present residents but also by many people

The long-serving the Revd Barrie Blowers pictured with wardens Tom Swinburn (left) and E.F.Raven (right) at an Annual Parochial Meeting.

with past connections with the area, and as a direct result the Normanton-by-Derby Local History Group was formed.

Vicars of St Giles' Church since it became a separate benefice in 1877

Revd	Appointed
Revd J.H.Lester MA	1877
Revd H.Price MA	1881
Revd J.Walmsley MA	1898
Revd J.Glass	1904
Revd G.E.A.Pargiter	1910
Revd R.Price MA	1920
Revd R.G.McAlpine MA	1936
Revd E.B.Bull MA	1943
Revd G.H.Stevens BD MTH	1949
Revd G.Seamer	1957
Revd Canon R.B.Blowers MA	1969

St Giles' Church

ALTHOUGH there is no mention of a church at Normanton in the Domesday Book, we know that a chapel was there in Norman times, perhaps built, or rebuilt as a result of the Manor of Normanton being given to the Canons of Darley Abbey in 1234.

The first historical mention comes in 1288 when the Abbot of Darley, as Rector of St Peter's, Derby, had a dispute with the parishioners of Normanton and Osmaston respecting repairs to their chapels. It was settled by an award of the Archdeacon of Derby that 'the Canons shall repair the chancels of the said chapels . . .' In Llewellyn Jewitt's *The Reliquary* there is a full description of this church just before it was demolished in 1861 to make way for a larger one. Evidently many alterations had been made over the years but several original Norman features still remained including a corbel table, with quaintly carved heads, running the length of the nave on both sides, and a carved stone which may have been the tympanum over the original doorway but by 1861 was set in the wall beside the south door.

This stone suffered further damage from the weather when it was again built into an outside wall near the base of the tower of the new building. It was brought inside when the church was enlarged in 1902-03 and set in the wall of the south porch. The stone has weathered badly and the carving is indistinct, but it is possible to see the Crucifixion represented in the centre. From the drawing made in 1861 it can be seen that the feet of Christ are shown separately side by side. This is understood to be an indication of pre-thirteenth-century work, as crossed feet were not introduced until the early thirteenth century.

The new church was opened amid great rejoicing on Tuesday, 13 May 1862, followed by services with guest preachers every evening of the following week, except Saturday. The *Derby Mercury* reported that the weather was good and the villagers had decorated the streets of the village with triumphal arches and garlands. Over the entrance to the churchyard was a floral design, painted in Old English — 'Enter into His gates with thanksgiving and into His courts with praise.'

At 11 o'clock in the morning, a procession assembled in the schoolroom consisting of the schoolchildren, the choristers, the clergy, committee, churchwardens, etc. On approaching the churchyard the choir commenced chanting the 24th Psalm and afterwards the 122nd Psalm. The choir and the lady organist who 'presided' at the harmonium were from St Peter's Church, Derby. Normanton was, of course, at that time part of the ancient parish of St Peter's, Derby, becoming a separate benefice in 1877.

The old church of St Giles', which was demolished in 1861. This illustration is from Jewitt's 'Reliquary', a copy of which is held in the Derby Local Studies Library.

Osmaston and Boulton were also daughter churches of St Peter's.

The new, but still small, church, was designed to seat 300 people. It consisted of what is now the side chapel and the part of the nave extending to the present centre aisle, along with the tower. The future increase in population had not been foreseen, as within a comparatively few years Normanton was no longer a small village surrounded by fields but was on the edge of a large built-up area. It became necessary to extend the church in 1893 and again in 1902-03, when a new nave and chancel were added to make the building its present size.

The first two windows in the north wall of the church were given by parishes where the Revd J.H.Lester (vicar 1877-1881) had held missions.

The next window, dated 1909, is in memory of Councillor Ottewell JP. The left light shows the injured deer of St Giles and is similar to a representation in the parish church of St Gilles, France, the first church founded by the monks of the Order of St Giles. The Derby 'Buck in the Park' is shown in the right-hand side.

There are memorial tablets on the north wall and a list of the people whose graves were displaced by the enlargement of the church. Also on the north wall are a World War One memorial transferred from the Macintosh Cable Company when their Sinfin Lane works closed in 1936, the World War Two

The Mothers' Union annual service was held on the second Monday in June, followed by a garden party at the Vicarage.

The Mothers' Union garden party. Despite the event being held in early June, the ladies are still attired in top coats. Hats, of course, were obligatory at any time of year.

A Mothers' Union group of the 1920s. The vicar is the Revd R. Price MA, who was at St Giles' from 1920 to 1936.

St Giles' Church, pictured at Easter 1993, showing the splendid winding path through the churchyard, such a lovely walk for wedding parties.

This steam locomotive proudly displays the fact that it is hauling carriages containing members of St Giles' Sunday School on their annual outing. The photograph was taken at Wirksworth Station in 1957.

Unveiling of the war memorial in the churchyard in July 1922. Lieutenant-General Sir F. G. Shaw performed the ceremony.

The opening of the extension to the St Giles' Church Centre in 1990.

memorial and the laid-up British Legion flags. There is a carved scroll on the pillar in the side chapel in memory of Gladys Taylor, a missionary with the Church Missionary Society in Tanganyika 1942-45 and a former member of the congregation.

The Victorian east window in the side chapel, representing the Ascension, is in memory of Anne Buck Radford, who died in 1882, and the alabaster reredos is in memory of her husband, Robert Radford of Park Hill, Normanton, who died in 1908.

The brass lectern in the main chancel was given on the occasion of the marriage of Francis Quekett Louch and Edith Maria Shaw (daughter of John Shaw of Normanton House) in 1885.

The vicar's prayer desk and the choir stalls were erected as a memorial to His Grace, the 8th Duke of Devonshire, Honorary Colonel of the 3rd Battalion,

Sherwood Foresters, and were unveiled by Lord Belper at a service on 14 July 1909. The subscribers included the Duke of Portland, the Duke of Newcastle, the Duke of Devonshire, Lord Belper, Lord Manvers, Major-General Talbot-Coke, Colonel Jelf, Colonel Sir Peter Walker, Sir Oswald Mosley and Sir Henry Bemrose.

The east window dates from 1947 and was put in as a thanksgiving memorial for victory in World War Two. The upper parts of the three central panels show the nativity, crucifixion and resurrection of Jesus, while the central light above sets forth the majesty of the Risen and Ascended Christ, based on *Revelations 1 v9-20*. St George, patron saint of England, is shown in the far left panel and on the far right St Giles, patron saint of the parish church, is portrayed with an arrow through his hand.

The church bell, dated 1712. It is inscribed D.W.Knight, Samuel Pegg, George Stenson, Churchwardens. J.Osborne. Vicar. "D.H." (Daniel Hadderley, bellfounder of Nottingham). The Revd J.Osborne was vicar of St Peter's, Derby, from 1664 to 1712 and was married at St Giles' on 5 May 1676.

At the base of the window the panels on the left have figures representing members of some of the services, with the inner panels showing the badges of military units such as the Royal Ordnance Corps, the Sherwood Foresters and the Auxiliary Territorial Service, which were closely associated with the parish during the war. The section on the right commemorates women who served in the armed forces and as munition workers.

The pulpit has alabaster panels and columns of Derbyshire stone with good examples of fossils. The impressive organ pipes over the panelling in front of the choir vestry are not part of the instrument but are purely ornamental. The plain octagonal font came from the old church and is believed to be of ancient origin.

The central light in the first window on the south wall is in memory of Lt.-Gen. William Raine Marshall, Commander-in-Chief of the Mesopotamian Expeditionary Force 1917-1919.

Along the south wall are various other Sherwood Forester memorials commemorating men who died in many different parts of the world. There is also a touching memorial to Rachel, wife of Colour Sergeant John Griffiths and schoolmistress of the 45th Regiment of Foot, who died of cholera in Neemuch, Bombay, in 1865, aged 22, and their two children, one of whom died aged nine days in 1864 and the

other in the following year, aged two months. Another memorial 'In memory of a Soldier's Wife' is to Florence Edith Shaw who died at the Royal Hospital, Dublin, in 1918 and was the wife of Lt.-Gen. the Rt Hon Sir Frederick Charles Shaw KGB. General Shaw was the second son of John Shaw of Normanton House, and in 1922 he unveiled the war memorial in the churchyard where wreaths are laid each year by members of ex-servicemen's organisations following the Remembrance Day service.

A plaque on the south wall, and others in the chancel, describe the Colours of the Sherwood Foresters which for many years hung in this church — a reminder that St Giles' was the regimental church with the vicar as their chaplain until Normanton Barracks closed in 1968. The Colours have now been removed to the Regimental Museum at Nottingham Castle for preservation. The latest Sherwood Forester plaque was placed on the south wall of the gallery and dedicated on 4 July 1993. It has been given by the Sherwood Foresters' Association in memory of all the Sherwood Foresters and their families who worshipped in St Giles' Church.

A carved oak chancel screen installed in 1947 to the memory of the Revd Robert Price (vicar 1920-36) now stands across the gallery at the back of the church.

The wrought-iron gas brackets are the fittings for

Normanton Vicarage.

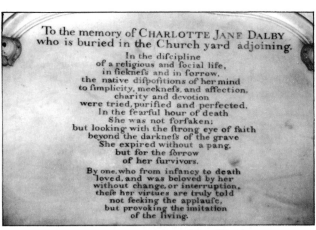

Tablet erected inside St Giles' Church.

the 'modern' gas lighting installed in 1903 and have been retained because of their historical interest.

The single church bell is inscribed 'W.D.Knight, Samuel Pegg, George Stenson, C.W. 1712 J Osborn Vic D.H.' D.H. seems to be for Daniel Hadderley, the bell founder of Nottingham and C.W. for churchwardens.

In the churchyard, as well as the graves of people from local families, and several soldiers, there are memorials to Sir Henry Howe Bemrose, died 1911. Canon Alfred Olivier, first vicar of St Thomas' church and afterwards first vicar of St James' church, died 1892, and the Revd William Hope, vicar of St Peter's Church, Derby, for 42 years, who died in 1889. After the churchyard was closed to new burials in 1897, due to lack of space, the Parish Council of the day purchased and laid out the cemetery on Stenson Road

for the use of residents of the ecclesiastical parish of Normanton. In 1975 all residents of Derby were given the right to be buried there and it ceased to be exclusively for the use of Normanton residents. It closed for new burials during the latter part of the 1980s. Since 1964 there has been a garden of remembrance in the churchyard for the burial of ashes.

St Stephen's Church, Sinfin, was built in 1935 as a daughter church to St Giles' but became a parish in its own right in 1979.

The church of St Giles' standing on the hill is both a landmark and evidence of many generations of Christian worship. But time has not stood still and the congregation now includes people from other countries who have made their home in Normanton and have become part of the changing local community.

Other Places Of Worship in Normanton-by-Derby

NORMANTON seems unique in that there are four places of worship in the same street — Village Street. As well as the Parish Church (rebuilt 1862), there is St George and All Soldier Saints (1920), the Church of God of Prophecy (1970s) — formerly the 'Old Sunday School,' and the First United Church of Jesus Christ (1980s) — formerly the Congregationalists. Close to lower Village Street is the St Thomas' Road Methodist Church (1908) and at the other end of the area is the former Sons of Temperance building (1915), now a Sikh temple, and the Gospel Hall on Walbrook Road.

St George and All Soldier Saints, Village Street

THE site which the Roman Catholic Church of St George's (as it is usually known) now occupies what was once farm land owned by Mr Peter Bresser of Rosedale Farm. It is alleged that here was the duck pond. The farmer donated the land for a chapel of ease as a thanks offering for the safe return of his son from World War One, and in memory of those who had lost their lives.

Farmer Bresser was a good friend of St Joseph's soccer team, who played their games at that time on land close to Pear Tree Station 'way out in the countryside'. Refreshments were provided for the team on match days from the farm house, next to the present social club on Village Street, everything being carried down to the pitch.

It was built very quickly, opening on 18 December 1920. Soldiers resident at the nearby Normanton Barracks no longer had quite so far to march for Sunday services, as up until then the nearest Roman Catholic church to Normanton was St Joseph's, off St Chad's Road near the town centre.

Unfortunately, due to the speed with which the building was constructed — a lack of damp-courses and solid foundations — cracks began to appear in the walls and the floor within a few years. Apparently the floor 'exuded a strange, powdery substance that was very attractive to the long dresses of the time'. Also, a lean was to be noticed to one side of the building, requiring the introduction of strong wooden supports which were installed on the tower side. Regrettably, legal and other associated problems caused the chapel to empty and eventually to close. It began to decay. The roof had fallen in and by 1925 the chapel had become an unattractive building.

The arrival in the parish of Canon Hargreaves was synonymous with the reopening of the chapel, which had almost entirely been rebuilt at a cost of between £3-4,000. It was noted that new housing estates were springing up around the area — and the faithful were called to services by a very distinctly tinny timbre of the bell. The ringer being a Mr Magee, who lived on the opposite side of the road. During World War Two, the ringing of the bell was reserved for warnings of invasion.

By 1 February 1945, St George and All Soldier Saints became a parish. About the same time, 45 Sackville Street was acquired as parish rooms and as the first lady chapel for the parish.

In 1955, Father Wakefield closed the church so that major repair work on the floor could be carried out and at the same time redecoration was done. During this time, Mass was said in the Cavendish Cinema.

The purchase of the old Co-operative Society's buildings next to the church took place in 1966 and they were demolished in the early 1970s.

More recently, in the 1980s, modernisation and improvement of the interior of the church has been carried out. Re-landscaping has been done and the nearby cottages have been renovated.

During the past couple of years there have been changes in the priests at St George's. A tragic accident caused the death, at the age of 92, of Father Briffa (a Jesuit) who had ministered in the parish for 20 years. He was riding his motor cycle from Valley Road on to the Ring Road, in the direction of his church, when the fatality occurred.

Father Briffa was born in Malta and served in World War One. He also saw action in World War Two, serving in Italy.

After 23 years in the parish, Father Mahar moved to a rural area (Brigg, Lincolnshire) in the autumn of 1992.

The Church of God of Prophecy, Village Street

THE building which now accommodates the Church of God of Prophecy was owned by the parish church until May 1976. A quite distinctive feature is the pattern incorporated into the roof. The blue-grey rectangular tiles are interspersed with three bands of red, almost circular tiles — fish-scale style.

In 1879 the property, on a plot measuring 354 square yards, was erected as a Sunday School and

Newspaper cutting from the 'Derby Evening Telegraph', 4 November 1929, showing the damage to St George's and All Soldier Saints in Village Street.

financed by Mr John Shaw of Normanton House, Village Street, at a cost of £500.

The opening of the new Sunday School was marked by the holding of the annual church tea party on the evening of New Year's Day 1880. Mr Shaw placed the building at the disposal of the vicar for the purposes of the church. It was described as 'a spacious and elegant building' designed by Messrs Giles and Brookhouse and built by the local builders Messrs Coxon and Edwards from the Balaclava Road area.

In his speech, Mr Shaw mentioned the great changes which had taken place in Normanton during the past five years, the great increase in population and the transformation which had taken place in the physical and geographical character of the district and the formation of Normanton into a separate parish.

Mr Dunkley, the former curate, also spoke, and Mr H.H.Bemrose gave the concluding address. Music was supplied by the church choir and members of the Normanton Musical Society were under the leadership of Mr L.Slater. The proceedings terminated about at 10.15pm.

During 1891, the building was conveyed to the vicar and wardens by Mr Shaw's trustees. Although Mr Shaw had built and given the building for church purposes, he had retained the right to use it when necessary for rent collecting purposes.

In 1921 a summer sale of work — held in the grounds of Normanton House (by this time the home of Mr and Mrs F.O.Ellison) — raised £1,000 in order to erect a parish hall and Sunday school. It had been found for a number of years that the 'Old Sunday School' had been unable to accommodate the children wishing to attend and the Council School had been

used for that purpose. It was said at the opening of the sale that the population was now 6,000 and that 2,000 more were expected.

Memories of the use of the premises go back to the 1920s. Many people recall the religious film shows — magic lantern shows — given by Mr Meadows (Sunday school superintendent) and later by Mr Broughton of Brunswick Street. At the Village Street end of the building was a raised tier of seats where the young people assembled. Apparently, they 'made a dive' for those seats. Films like the *Pilgrim's Progess* were shown.

A plan from the early 1920s shows the gallery as being 18ft 1in by 5ft high at the back with a platform 14ft by 6ft 5in opposite to it. Also shown is a kitchen 12ft by 6ft 3in. It is understood that this kitchen was pulled down and replaced by a new building consisting of a kitchen and committee room in 1933. It is also believed that coal fires were used in the main hall up to that time. The party wall with 167 Village Street shows evidence of fireplace openings having been bricked up and the out-buildings at the rear were most likely to have been a coal house.

Sunday schools and other church activities continued here until the onset of World War Two.

The 'Old Hall', as it was usually known, was requisitioned on 29 March 1940 under the Emergency Powers Act and was used by the Army as a store. Payment was £40 per year. The small room at the back of the building was used by the Primary School as additional classrooms space. The Girl Guides used this room for their meetings and members recall having to move the iron-legged desks around to create enough space.

The former Sunday School building in Village Street, now used by the Church of God of Prophecy.

From the 1950s the organisations associated with the Church began using the building once more, in particular the Kindergarten Sunday School.

Extensive repairs were carried out in 1966-67, including rewiring, a new floor for the main hall, new roofing to the committee room and kitchen, and a new ceiling to the committee room. The front wall was rebuilt and toilets were constructed in the side porch. The cost of this work was £1,588.

The signatories to the purchase document dated 20 May 1976 were Charles Glennis Hawkins, Alfred Washington Gums, Joseph Nathaniel Powell and Adrian Laurence Varleck of Tennessee, USA.

Even after the sale of the property, the Kindergarten Sunday School were allowed to use the larger of the two halls for several months for their afternoon meetings, pending the completion of the new church centre.

The new church has altered the exterior of the building, namely, making the main entrance straight off Village Street — with steps leading up.

St Thomas' Road Methodist Church, St Thomas' Road
ACCORDING to *Bagshaw's Directory* of 1846 it is stated that 'the Primitive Methodists have a chapel much older' than the one of 1844 erected by the Independents.

Apparently, Sarah Kirkland the daughter of a Mugginton farmer, became a well-known figure of early Primitive Methodism in the district and she began a society which was established after the meetings at the Mercaston camp in June 1816.

The first meeting place in Old Normanton was a barn in what was then known as Cabbage Square — now Browning Street — at its junction with Village Street, a place visible until 1966.

The years rolled by and Normanton began to grow — the Primitive Methodists looked for a new site and erected an iron building for a school and chapel on Sackville Street in 1891. This was the year that Queen Victoria came to Derby to lay the foundation stone for the new Infirmary.

However, the Society was soon looking towards a newer and larger building. A site for the new building was found when farmer Berresford of Balfour Road offered a piece of land for sale. The Society purchased this for £515. The architect for the project was a Mr P.Kirkland and thereafter local builders were invited to tender to build the new chapel. The successful proposal was from a Mr J.Young who quoted £745 for the job — the cost of heating and lighting being extra.

Two stone-laying ceremonies were held — the first on August Bank Holiday Monday, 1907 (at that time, August Monday was at the beginning of the month) and also on 31 August 1907.

The cost of the installation of the heating came to £33 and it cost £21 for the lighting — bringing the full cost, which included other expenses, to £1,314. Many different ways of raising the cash were devised, including the presentation of a trowel to all those who subscribed £5 and over.

Saturday, 4 January 1908 was the day of the opening ceremony and this was performed by Mrs Boden of The Friary, Friar Gate — who was president of the British Women's Temperance Association.

The iron building which had served so well on the site in Sackville Street was subsequently sold for £40 for use as Crewton Mission, a daughter of Alvaston Church. The land in Sackville Street was put up for sale at a figure of £200. The debt incurred in the building of the chapel was not finally cleared until 1938, despite much effort being made to settle it.

By 1966, it had become evident that an extension to the Church was necessary. Builders' quotations were reviewed and one was accepted in August and Saturday, 5 November was set for the stone-laying ceremony. The opening and dedication of the new church took place in July 1967. A large vestry was built at the back of the church and the 'old church' was made into a large hall, with staging. Some of the finance for this extension came from the sale of Dale Road Methodist Church, Lower Dale Road, New Normanton.

A Primitive Methodist Church had been erected beside the 'New School Room' in Lower Dale Road in 1902. The organ later installed in the church is understood to have originally been in the church of St Martin-in-the-Fields, London. It was a building of considerable size, with a balcony, and enjoyed good membership for many years. But the problems of cleaning and maintenance and eventually a dwindling congregation proved a headache. The cost of heating, by means of a coke-fired boiler, was escalating. After much heart searching and discussion, the premises were sold to the Serbian Orthodox Church. Members dispersed to other churches, including St Thomas' Road Methodists.

A new pipe organ was opened and dedicated in April 1976 and a recital on the instrument was given by Mr David S. Johnson of Derby.

Over the years the congregation of St Thomas' Road Methodists has been augumented by members from other churches in the vicinity which have closed, including Green Hill Methodists, Old Normanton Congregational and Rose Hill Methodists.

The church still has many organisations associated with it and continues to thrive.

Sons of Temperance, Duncan Road, now Shri Radvidass Bhawan Temple

THE foundation stone laying ceremony at the Sons of Temperance Hall was carried out on 1 May 1915. A large number of spectators were present in addition to the dignitaries who included the Mayor and Mayoress (Councillor and Mrs J.Hill), Mrs Henry Boden (president of the British Womens' Temperance Association), Sir Thomas Roe MP, Mr J.H.Thomas MP, Mr A.C.Bonas (president of the Derby and District Band of Hope Union) and Mr T.Harpur (president of Derby Temperance Society).

The chairman, Mr Walter Davies JP, spoke of the aims of the Sons of Temperance and its origins: "The organisation was started in 1855 and the drink traffic was the chief devastator of the age. It required a strong agency to combat it. The growing needs of Derby placed them under the obligation of building a Hall."

At that time there were 5,250 insurance members on their books, a considerable increase on the figures of a few years previously. An appeal was made to the public to subscribe £300 — making a quarter of the cost of the building.

A number of foundation stones were laid — by the Mayor, Sir Thomas Roe MP, Mr T.Harpur, Mrs Henry Boden, Mr J.H.Thomas MP and Mr A.C.Bonas.

In his speech, MP 'Jimmy' Thomas commented that 'drink was as much a danger to the mansion as to the cottage'.

The building was designed to accommodate 350 people. The architect was Mr G.Cash and the builders, Messrs Barker, Cooper & Sons.

Little is known about activities in the building since that time except that a parochial gathering connected with St Giles' Church was held in the Sons of Temperance Hall on 13 February 1920, when Mr Giles Austin spoke on the social side of church work.

Also, in the 1940s, Pleasant Sunday Afternoons operated at the Sons of Temperance. An orchestra consisting of Aubrey Stafford (leader), George Platts, Bill Poynton (piano), Trevor Poynton, Ernie Place, Mr Jackson (violin), Frank Garratt, Mr and Mrs Borsley and their son and daughter, Jim Mace (drums) and Reg Smith (bass), entertained the patrons.

An advertisement published in September 1941 announced that at Normanton PSA, Sons of Temperance Hall, Walbrook Road and Duncan Road, 'one minute from The Cavendish', on Sunday, 21 September 1941 at 3pm, the 30th anniversary service would be held. The speaker was to be Mr P.J.Noel-Baker, MP on the subject of 'Nansen, The League and its future'. The chairman was Alderman W.R.Raynes.

After World War Two, several out-buildings were let to businesses such as a car repair firm and also to the St Thomas' Scout Group. The hall itself has been home to Townswomen's Guild meetings and to Women's Institutes as well as the rehearsal room of the Good Companion's Stage Society.

It appears that the building was sold to the Sikh community during the 1980s and the premises now serve as Shri Radvidass Bhawan Temple.

Wesleyan Methodist Chapel, Sinfin Lane, Sinfin

THIS was opposite the site of Barker's Farm at the junction of Sinfin Lane and Grampian Way, Sinfin Moor. In the mid-nineteenth century there was concern that the agricultural labourers of the Sinfin district had no church that they could easily attend. The nearest places of worship were at Barrow-on-Trent and Normanton-by-Derby. A chapel was built in 1868 by Mr Mather of Sinfin House Farm at his own expense, on land owned by him just inside the Normanton boundary.

By 1949 the building was unused — being derelict

Cottages in Browning Street which were demolished in 1966. One was once used as a Primitive Methodist meeting house.

and vandalised. At this time the 119th Sinfin, St Stephen's Scout Group were looking for suitable headquarters. The Scoutmaster, Ron Adamson, was put in touch with a Mr Mather who had been willed the property. Mr Mather agreed to the Scouts making use of the property and they then set about the renovation of the building. This was used by the troop for some years until a decline in the population caused the closure of the group.

The building was later taken over by Sinfin Moor Football Club, who made use of it until it was demolished to make way for housing development on the large Sinfin Moor development.

St Stephen's Church, Sinfin

FOLLOWING the building of the new estate at Sinfin and the consequent increase in population, the Vicar of Normanton, the Revd R.Price, was concerned about the provision of a place of worship for the people living there and was instrumental in the church being built.

The foundation stone for St Stephen's Church, daughter church to Normanton, was laid on 1 June 1935 by Mrs Price, wife of the Vicar of Normanton. Previously there had been no building owned by the church in the area, but Miss Betty Neasham (later Mrs Cartwright) had established a Sunday School there which met in the day school.

On 14 September 1935, the new building was filled to capacity for its opening and dedication by the Archdeacon of Derby (the Ven Spencer Noakes) assisted by Canon Cooper and the Revd R.Price. St Giles' choir led the singing and the organ was played by Mr G.H.Taylor.

The building cost £2,200, and for some years a group of people from St Giles' collected weekly amounts from people on the estate who had made promises of money towards the cost of the church. It was a dual purpose building, being used as a church for services and as a hall when the sanctuary was closed off by a screen.

Four years later, an iron-clad church hall was erected by Austins the builders of Stenson Road. It came from a site near Ascot Drive and cost £360. The hall, officially called 'The Social Hall' was opened by the Archdeacon of Derby on 30 September 1939,

and the ceremony was followed by tea and entertainment — all for the cost of 9d. During World War Two the building was taken over by the Army.

In 1976 extra rooms were built on, but three years later the congregation had the vision for the present Family Centre which cost £42,000. It was officially opened by the Bishop of Derby on 20 March 1981 after he had consecrated St Stephen's as a Parish Church. St Stephen's had become a separate parish and benefice in 1979, and the Revd Martin White, already serving as curate, was inducted as the first vicar of the church in April 1980.

Stipendiary Curates
1935-37 Revd A.Tonge
1938-43 Revd H.M.Woodward
1943-46 Revd Eric Thomas Allen
1946-50 Revd Billy Bould
1951-52 Revd Albert Saul Shammash
1952-54 Revd William Hugh Cyril Simmonds
1954-58 Revd Frederick Herbert Sisley
1959-60 Revd David Anthony Quine
1960-63 Revd Derek Henry Kingham
1963-65 Revd Gordon Cresswell Delevingne
1965-71 Revd Eric Stott
1972-77 Revd Don Wrapson
1978-80 Revd Martin White

Incumbents
1980-88 Revd Martin White
1988-91 Revd David Ashton
1991-   Revd Timothy Price

First United Church of Jesus Christ (Apostolic), Village Street, formerly Old Normanton Congregational Church.

THE foundation stone of Old Normanton Congregational Church on Village Street was laid on 19 June 1869 by James Allport, Esq. The church was first opened for Divine Worship on 19 January 1870. The cost of the building was £500.

The church consisted of the main body — with one vestry. Around it on two sides there was a yard, with gardens on the eastern side. Entrance was via a large wooden porch on the western corner. The church was lit by gas lamps — which had to be lighted by taper. The heating was by means of a large coke stove on the eastern side. Over the original screen were written the words 'Praise waiteth for thee O God in Zion' with further texts on either side. The rostrum was a reading desk with open rails around it, thereby giving the preacher lots of room to walk about. The chapel seated about 200 persons. The school at the rear which connected with the main building by means of lifting shutters, could hold nearly 100 more.

The *Derby Mercury* of January 1870 reported that the Chapel was 'a simple building in Early English Style of architecture, the principal architectural features externally being trifori headed and plate traceried windows; high pitched gables and a timber-framed and slated bell turret and porch. The architect was Mr Tait of Leicester'.

A communion service, consisting of silver plates,

cups and flagon, was presented by Mrs Frances Goodale in 1871.

In June 1882, a committee was formed 'for the purpose of managing the chapel'. It was a mission church sponsored by Victoria Street and London Road Church. The Committee was made up of the following: Messrs Brentnall, J.Cooper, B.Cooper, J.Cottam, R.Eden, Harding, Hulme, J.Hunt, H.Kinnerley, A.Laing, W.Smith and Stevenson.

An estimate was obtained in July 1882 for an iron gateway with a gas lamp over it. The church's first organ was, in fact, an harmonium and Mr Samuel Lane played it.

By February 1904, records name people involved with the church as Messrs Porter, Stone, Radford, Wheatley, Smith and Barton. Student pastors and a Mr Kirby were preachers.

On 27 October 1904 the mother church — Victoria Street — offered to appoint a minister to work Old Normanton and Crewton jointly. At this time the organ was played by Mr Will Stone, Mr Barton and Mr Eden.

The Revd D.J.Price was appointed minister of the church in 1905 and was responsible for the morning service. Mr Porter took the evening service.

In the seven years up to 1912, several families left the church — namely Stone, Cooper, Bryant and Bradley — to make new homes for themselves in Canada and Australia. New families began to attend the church — Graham; Wheeler, Barton, Worrall, Glover and Degg.

A new set of proposals for the running of the church was drafted out by Victoria Street Congregational Church — that the Old Normanton Committee should not spend more than 30 shilings (£1.50) in any one quarter without the consent of the mother church and that a written report be presented quarterly to the executive.

The minister of Victoria Street, the Revd I.R.Ackroyd, visited the chapel for the Sunday School anniversaries.

A great feature about this time were the Saturday afternoon and Whit Monday rambles for young and old to Ingleby, Breedon and Melbourne. An annual outing was made by brake to Windley. The Mutual Improvement Society met during the winter evenings and the older people read and discussed papers.

More new people joined the congregation — Messrs Leaton, Frost and G.Clarke, Lawley and Miss Hobbs and Miss Wardman. Mr and Mrs Degg were responsible for the Band of Hope.

The British Women's Association entertained and gave tea to the wives and mothers of those serving in the Forces during World War One.

Under the secretaryship of Mr F.Tabberer, estimates were obtained in April 1923 for lighting the church by electricity. About the same time, Derby Corporation made enquiries about purchasing the land to the east side of the church for an arterial road.

Responsibility for their own finance was granted by the deacons at Victoria Street in February 1925 and Mr Glover became the treasurer. New members were Messrs Brooks, Blythe and Yeomans, but unfortunately congregations dwindled and the work of the church declined.

Rumours had abounded for some time that the church was to be pulled down. However, in April 1926 the Revd T.Rook reported at a church meeting that only the gardens were required for the new road. Membership again dwindled in 1928 when it was rumoured that the Corporation wished to purchase the church buildings.

After going to arbitration in early 1931, £300 was received for the land adjoining the church — £750 having been the highest figure offered. At this time Miss K.Worrall was the church secretary.

Under the leadership of Mr F.W.Worrall — from March 1934 — a new room was built on to the east side the church, the doorway blocked up and a new entrance made from Kenilworth Avenue. The money received from the sale of the land financed this project.

In July 1937, the gift of an organ was made by Carlton Road Congregational Church — £60 being paid for the overhaul and the fixing of an electric blower.

At the end of 1949, lay pastor Worrall resigned after 15 years. The new lay pastor, Mr Todd, was welcomed to the church on 29 March 1950.

The church was registered for the solemnising of marriages in 1958.

Two new windows were fixed in the church during 1960 and a great improvement was made. The secretaryship of the church was taken over in late 1965 — almost 40 years after her mother had taken up the same position — by Miss K.Louch. Re-roofing of the main building was carried out in September 1965.

As the Centenary approached, the membership was decreasing and the congregation was dwindling. By 1972, the Congregationalists had merged to form the United Reformed Church.

In the 1980s, moves were made to dispose of the church building but Derby City Council would not allow a change of use of the premises.

During the time leading up to closure of the Old Normanton Congregationalist Church in January 1984, the building was being shared with the new occupants, the First United Church of Jesus Christ (Apolistic). Some considerable time was spent in improving the interior and exterior appearance of the building and tidying up the surroundings by the new owners.

The War Years

THE notice in the *Derby Evening Telegraph* was from St Giles' Church. It reminded parishioners that evensong had been brought forward to 3.30pm because of blackout restrictions. Underneath was the terse message: 'Don't stop praying for peace.' The date was 9 September 1939, and the conflict we now know as World War Two had just begun. It was less than 20 years since the memorial to those lost in World War One — 'the war to end all wars' — had been erected in the churchyard. Now Normanton, along with the rest of Britain, had to face again the trials of war. This time the Home Front was to contribute much more to the struggle.

War was not unexpected. An uneasy peace with Germany had prevailed for several years. By 1938, Civil Defence workers had been mobilised and plans made for air-raid precautions and evacuation. Even so, some people refused to admit the possibility of war. Civil Defence workers in Normanton tell of being ridiculed when distributing pamphlets on air-raid precautions, and some people even refused to take gas masks. On 1 September 1939, Germany breached the Polish frontier, blackout restrictions came into force, evacuation began and even the most hopeful realised that war was inevitable. On the morning of Sunday, 3 September, the Prime Minister broadcast to the nation that the country was at war with Germany.

During the first few months of the war, the civilian population was organised for defence against the enemy. The principal threat was seen as being from air attack. Domestic air-raid shelters were delivered and installed. These were called Anderson shelters after the Home Secretary, Sir John Anderson. They consisted of a shell of corrugated iron buried to a depth of several feet, with soil heaped over the curved roof. Many people remember them with horror as damp, claustrophobic places, prone to flooding in wet weather.

Amazingly, quite a few still survive in Normanton, often rebuilt after the war as garden sheds! Some public shelters were provided, one being on the corner of Kenilworth Avenue and Stenson Road. Shelters were built in the grounds of Homelands, both for the use of that school and for the nearby Normanton Council School. Former Homelands pupils recall cultivating the earth over these shelters to produce vegetables to supplement the school dinners!

A more active defence against air attack was provided by a barrage balloon and anti-aircraft guns being located on Normanton Recreation Ground. People living close by were alarmed one night when there was a loud explosion as if a bomb had been dropped. It transpired that the anti-aircraft guns had been replaced by naval guns which, being much more powerful, were quite capable of shaking nearby houses. A similar gun was sited in a field near Stenson Road with consequent disturbance to residents of the Sunnyhill district.

Perhaps the most hated part of the defence system was the smoke screen. Units, consisting of a fuel reservoir, a tall chimney and a lid, were placed every few yards along the principal roads of the district. They were fuelled by waste oil and when lit, gave off clouds of thick smoke. The idea was to shroud the district in an artificial fog, in order to hide major landmarks from aircraft. The smell was terrible and permeated houses, tainting food, whilst the oily dirt in the atmosphere soiled curtains and furnishings. One lady recalls lighting joss sticks in an attempt to disguise the smell but without success. Several people remember the unfortunate soldiers in charge of the smoke screen as being permanently covered in a black, greasy deposit.

A tragic incident occurred in connection with the smoke screen in 1940. A group of children were playing around one of the units on Coleridge Street, and one of the boys was badly burnt. Sadly, he died some months later.

There were two schools in Normanton at the beginning of the war: Homelands (now Village Community School) and Normanton Council School (now Normanton Village Infant School). Both schools closed as a temporary measure. There was some evacuation of pupils, mostly into rural areas of Derbyshire. Homelands reopened within a few weeks, but Normanton Council School remained closed to pupils until January 1940 and then opened only on a part-time basis. It was not fully functional until March 1940. In the interim, pupils were taught in small groups, mostly in private houses.

When full-time education did recommence, there were many disruptions. Air-raid drill had to be carried out — first as a practice and later for actual warnings. Morning attendance was often as low as 25 per cent as children were kept at home after night raids. There were staff changes as members joined the forces or undertook other war work, and many unscheduled closures due to various crises. Later on in the war, the schools were used as reception centres for evacuees from the London area.

A vital part of the war effort took place in the home where housewives in particular bore the burden of 'stretching' the food rations to keep the family adequately fed. Some ladies attended cookery classes at the nearby Pear Tree School. Here they were introduced to such delights as Spam rissoles and scrambled dried egg. One lady remembers that the high spot of the week was if she managed to get a rabbit 'off the ration' to share with her next-door

Normanton's Civil Defence workers outside Homelands School during World War Two.

neighbour. Another vividly recollects queuing for almost two hours at the Co-op grocery for two ounces of cooked ham!

Gradually an efficient Civil Defence organisation began to evolve in Normanton. The ARP headquarters was in a building, now demolished, near Normanton House on Village Street. There were several other posts throughout the district, one being in the basement of the Cavendish cinema where, according to an ex-warden, they shared the accommodation with the mice.

A First-Aid post was set up in one of the classrooms at Normanton Council School. This was manned at night mainly by part-time Civil Defence workers. At first they had to report for duty every time there was an air-raid warning. This meant that they could be on duty for several nights at a stretch, perhaps until six in the morning, and still have to do a full day's work. Eventually a more workable rota system was arranged. Later, they merged with the Rescue Service and were relocated near the Vulcan, in a building which later became a Police Station.

When the war began it was expected that the greatest danger would be from high-explosive bombs. While it was true that these were responsible for most air-raid casualties, it was in fact fire that did most of the damage. At that time fire services were localised and connections for hydrants varied from district to district. This caused problems if pumps from another area were sent to help out in an emergency. In August 1941, the existing fire authorities were merged into one — the National Fire Service. Steps were also taken to ensure that every factory and street appointed fire-

watchers. Emergency water supplies in the form of static water tanks appeared, one being at the bottom of Walbrook Road.

Some extra fire stations were provided in addition to the principal ones. One — complete with pole — was opened in the stables behind the Sherwood Hotel. It was staffed mainly by part-time members of the Auxiliary Fire Service. A big advantage of this location was that, when it was quiet, the men could slip away for a drink in the bar. A bell was connected to provide a discreet warning should anyone in authority choose to visit the station!

Many men were recruited into the Local Defence Volunteers, later known as the Home Guard. In the early days they were very short of equipment. One local man still recalls his disgust at being expected to drill with a dummy wooden rifle — especially as he had left important work on munitions to attend the practice. However, as the war progressed, proper equipment and uniforms were provided. The scout hut at the top of Coleridge Street was used for Home Guard activities. A rifle range was set up in the corridor, the men firing into a bank of sandbags at one end.

The war years brought an increase in military activity to Normanton. The army barracks at the top of Sinfin Lane had long been a familiar landmark in the district. Now it became the scene of much greater movement. In addition there was now an army camp at Sunnyhill. Some local people provided accommodation for wives of soldiers from the camp, so that they could be with their husbands during short spells off duty. Friendships between hosts and

Members of the National Fire Service pictured at the Sherwood Hotel, Normanton, in 1945.

'lodgers' often survived for many years after the war. There was also some billeting of soldiers on local households.

Situated as it is in close proximity to the Rolls-Royce factory, it was expected that Normanton would be in the target area for air attack. In the event there were only a few bombing incidents in the district — indeed, Derby as a whole escaped intensive attack.

In August 1940, bombs dropped in Stenson Road demolished two bungalows. Fortunately the occupants were in their air-raid shelters, otherwise they would probably have been killed. The force of the explosion flung them across the shelter and one lady received serious leg injuries and subsequently had to have part of her leg amputated. In April 1941, houses and bungalows were badly damaged in Littleover Lane.

The heaviest raid on Derby occurred in January 1941, when a string of bombs fell on the Derby Lane/Kenilworth Avenue area. Four houses were demolished in Offerton Avenue and others damaged. Some families were still in their homes and several people were killed. These included a mother and her baby, and a teenage girl and her mother.

Two houses were destroyed on the corner of Derby Lane, and there was extensive damage to property in Derby Lane, Laurel Bank, Kenilworth Avenue, and Village Street. Several people were trapped in Anderson shelters at the back of Kenilworth Avenue, when earth and rubble were blown against the entrances. Most of the damage to houses was caused

when debris blasted skywards came down through the roofs. One lady remembers that it was a brilliant moonlit night — as she discovered when she went into her bedroom and saw the moon shining through a hole in the ceiling! There are several accounts of 'near misses' when beds only recently vacated were showered with rocks and concrete.

For those who experienced it, the shock of being involved in an air-raid is still vividly recalled after 50 years. Several people remember their terror when, after the Derby Lane bombing, the sirens went again the same night. Fortunately there was no repeat attack. One man, who later joined the RAF, acknowledges that in all his five years in the service, he was never as frightened as he was that night in Normanton.

Although many Normanton residents remember the war as a time of anxiety, when they had the worry of the safety of their family at home as well as for those in the armed forces, the majority of people speak of the great sense of community of that time. There was a certain satisfaction in enduring together all the privations and dangers. As one lady summed it up: "I wouldn't like to go through it again, I wouldn't like another war, but I think I am glad that it was in my time."

In May 1945, Germany surrendered to the Allies. The official capitulation of Japan was signed on 2 September the same year. World War Two was finally over.

Two war memorials may be seen in St Giles' Church, the Royal British Legion Roll of Honour

The Home Guard parade down Coleridge Street.

Queuing for gas masks outside Normanton School in 1938.

and the Commemorative East Window.

Sadly, yet another war memorial was to appear in Normanton. On 12 June 1982, a local man, serving in the Royal Marines, was killed in action in the Falklands War. A plaque in his memory is sited in the Main Hall at the Village Community School.

Perhaps it is still just as important that we 'don't stop praying for peace'.

Bomb crater in Derby Lane, Normanton, after the air-raid of January 1941, Derby's heaviest of the war.

Schools in Normanton

THE earliest records to be found of schools in the village of Normanton are recorded in *White's Directory* of 1857, in which we are informed that a school was erected by subscription in 1851. It was for boys, girls and infants, to hold 80 pupils although only about 50 attended. The school mistress was Anne Watkinson.

By the 1864 edition of *White's Directory*, we are told there was a National School — a term introduced following the 1861 Report of the Duke of Newcastle's Commission to 'inquire into the present state of popular education in England, and to consider and report what measures, if any, are required for the extension of sound and cheap elementary instruction to all classes of the people.' (*An Introduction to the History of English Education since 1800* by Curtis and Boultwood. Reprinted 1970.) Normanton's school mistress was Miss Elizabeth Evans.

The 1871 *Wright's Directory* states that there is a 'mixed National School'.

The late Mr James Tabberer recalled that the school was situated in buildings opposite the Norman Arms and that the children paid twopence for the privilege of attending.

An announcement made on 16 January 1878 stated that a Miss Kinsey had opened the 'Clifton House School for Young Ladies' and was preparing to receive a limited number of resident and daily pupils. The school was at the Stenson Road end of Village Street and is presently the doctor's surgery (formerly the Derby Co-operative Society's Store). It is not clear whether the building was purpose-built as a school or was built as a private house and altered later.

Education Nationally

The 1868 General Election resulted in Mr Gladstone becoming Prime Minister. Mr W.E.Forster, MP for Bradford (vice-president of the Education Department) was given the responsibility for the introduction of a new Education Bill. A complete survey of the educational needs of all districts was to be made. School Boards were to be elected by those on the burgesses roll of boroughs and by the ratepayers in the country. Thus the Elementary Education Act of 1870 was born. The School Boards were to consist of a minimum of five and a maximum of 15 members. Women could vote for members and they could sit on the Board.

School Boards were allowed to levy a local rate for the building of the schools and they could acquire land, raise a loan for the building of schools and could make education compulsory in their area.

Two additional Education Acts were made during the ensuing decade: Lord Sandon's Act of 1876 raised the Government grant to managers of voluntary schools; and the Mundella Act, 1880 enabled School Boards to frame attendance bye-laws.

Developments In Primary Education In Normanton

During January 1876, a meeting of the ratepayers was held in the old school room and the Revd J.H.Lester (vicar), Mr John Shaw (land agent), Mr William Briggs (solicitor), Mr Charles Brentnall (maltster) and Mr Oakley were elected for a School Board.

The first meeting of the School Board was held on 24 Febuary 1876, taking place in the (Old) School Room on Village Street. Mr Shaw was elected chairman and the Revd J.H.Lester was vice-chairman. A resolution was passed 'that a site for a new school should be found between the village of Old Normanton and New Normanton — because of the increasing population.'

Three years later, Mr S.H.Evans (surgeon) was substituted for Mr Oakley on the board and by April 1879, the Education Department in Whitehall had sanctioned the purchase of a plot of land measuring 1,400 square yards at six shillings (30p) per yard from Mr Shaw of Normanton House.

A mixed school, to accommodate 150 children, with a space adjoining the parsonage on Cabbage Square was designed by Messrs Giles and Brookhouse. A local firm of builders — Messrs Coxon and Edwards — agreed to erect the school at a cost of £1,350.

On 31 December 1879, an advertisement appeared in the *Derby Mercury* and other newspapers for a certificated master and an infant mistress. Applications stating age, salary required and previous employment (with testimonials) were to be sent to the clerk of the board not later than the 11 January 1880.

Normanton Board School

Interviews for the post of headmaster of Normanton Board School took place at the Sunday School on 27 January 1880 and Mr William Powell BA (London) was appointed with effect from Lady Day — 25 March. Miss Elizabeth Duddell was appointed the infant and sewing mistress. It was resolved that the school fees should be: Infants, 2d per week; 2nd to 4th Standard, 3d per week; above 4th Standard, 4d per week.

On 26 April 1880, Normanton Board School was opened. An entry in the school log book for that day states: 'I, William Powell, master, have this day opened Normanton Board School (mixed department) and admitted 16 boys and 21 girls.'

An investigation into the operation of the school was carried out by Her Majesty's Inspectors on 4 October 1880 and it was reported that the children were being carefully taught by Mr Powell and his staff. 'The work on slate and paper was particularly

A group thought to be of children from Normanton School, date unknown but probably around the turn of the century.

good. Subjects well taught were Arithmetic, Reading, Writing, Grammar, Recitation and Needlework but School Drill should be introduced.'
School Log Book

Mrs Shaw gave the prizes and the school board provided the certificates for what appears to be the first occasion when these were distributed on Friday, 2 December 1881.

In January 1890, the Log Book records that 'owing to the inconvenience of getting children to supply themselves with the necessary school books and materials, the Board has decided to make a small increase in the school fee to cover the cost of a free supply of all school requisites, except slate pencils. After today (13th) the fees will be as follows: Infants — under 5 years, 2d; Infants — over 5 years, 3d; Older children, 4d and 5d.'

A presentation was made during this month to Mr Powell and his wife, the former Miss Duddell, in celebration of their recent marriage. The presentation was made at the school, by Mr Edwin Parker, clerk to the board.

Eighteen months later — in September 1891 — free education was adopted, dependant on regular attendance.

In September 1894, new furniture was provided. It consisted of 18 dual kindergarten desks, five teachers' desks with high chairs, two 12ft school desks, one blackboard stand and two cupboards. During this year, a further classroom was added.

The late Mr Joe Harrison — at the school around 1899 — recalled: "The infant classroom was the room on the left-hand side of the entrance with an open fire place and a coal fire."

It is noted from the Log Book that over the next four years celebrations and holidays were the order of the day. Starting with the Diamond Jubilee, there followed Queen Victoria's birthday, the departure of Reservists from Normanton Barracks for South Africa, and on 1 February 1901, a 'special service in commemoration of the death of Queen Victoria was conducted by the Vicar, at the School'.

Normanton Council School

The 1902 Education Act abolished the School Boards and established Local Education Authorities run by the Councils. In September 1903, therefore, Normanton Board School became Normanton Council School. The number of staff had increased and as well as Mr Powell there were the Misses E.Nicholson, M.A.Critchlow, E.Wragg, H.Critchlow, W.Adey, F.Critchlow and M.Henshall. The subjects on the curriculum consisted of reading, writing, composition, spelling, poetry, recitation, history, geography, science, needlework, object lessons, cookery, woodwork, singing, marching and physical drill.

Big celebrations must have gone on in Normanton for the Coronation of King George V in June 1911. The school was closed for a week and, as well as the presentation of medals to the children of the parish by Mrs Powell, there was a church service followed

Normanton Council School group of the early 1900s.

by a march to Mr Clayton's field for tea and sports. The over 60s had a meat tea in the Church Sunday School and 300 other adults had a meat tea in the Council School. The Parish Council's bill for the day was £34 9s 0d.

Two events are interesting towards the end of World War One. On 29 January 1918, the children were given a holiday in the afternoon so that they could see the visit of the tank to Derby and another afternoon's holiday was allowed in September to 'permit the children to pick blackberries for the government'. The end of the war was celebrated by a four-day closure from 12 November 1918.

The building is remembered as consisting of two classrooms where the hall is now. The areas were partitioned by a red curtain. The internal windows enabled Mr Powell to see clearly into every classroom. Several pictures were to be seen around the hall — one showed King George V and Queen Mary, the other a soldier standing next to his field gun. On the far wall were the words 'Knowledge is Power' and on the opposite wall 'Power is Strength'.

Mr Powell resigned from his post on 31 March 1923 — 43 years after he opened the school. He was known as 'Ginger' Powell to the children (probably because of his red beard) and is remembered as being short, well-built and smart in appearance. It is said that 'his vigour and thoroughness impressed itself on the minds of Normanton's young.'
Some Account of the History of Normanton by Derby and Its Church Harrison.

"He was strict and his cane always lay across his desk," remembers Mr Cedric Allsopp, whose schooling began in January 1911.

Mr Powell — who had always taken an interest in the public, social and religious affairs of the village — died at Lake House on 26 December 1929.

With the appointment of the new headmaster, Mr Cecil Oldham on 30 April 1923, changes took place around the school. A new timetable was tried out in the infant classes, giving shorter lessons and more varied arrangements. The children attended Reginald Street Baths for swimming and in 1925 a four-valve wireless set was installed.

Class sizes in September, 1925 were:

Class 1 — 64
Class 2 — 64
Class 3 — 64
Class 4 — 64
Class 5 — 60
Class 6 — 61
Class 7 — 60 Total 437

Normanton Infant School

As can be seen from the above numbers, the school was beginning to become rather full. The 'Becket' buildings — later known as 'the West Wing' were put in place in 1927 behind the old school. As the Ministry of Education would not approve them as an extension to the existing school, Normanton Infant School was created. There were four classrooms and two cloakrooms. Miss G. Orme was appointed

This time we can be quite definite about the date. The slate board clearly says that this group of Normanton Council School children were posed for the camera in 1911.

headmistress and Mr Oldham was responsible for the older children in the main building.

Miss Orme (head 1927-1934) remembers: "During my service, an extra classroom and head and staff room were added. All the floors of these wooden buildings were of planks and the wind blew in. Eventually these were covered with lino, which was most satisfactory. I was told on my appointment that the buildings were guaranteed for thirty-five years. For the first few years the classrooms were lit by Aladdin oil lamps, which frequently blew out. There were no lights in the cloakrooms.

"On Empire Days and other special occasions the two schools met in the playground and we danced round the maypole or displayed gymnastics and other activities.

"There were no school dinners but a voluntary scheme for milk was organised. At one time the school overflowed again and the Sunday School on Village Street was used, as was the old Village Hall where the juniors had a domestic science class. We also held our school concerts there.

"I served under the county authority for a year and two months when, on extension of the Borough's boundary, we came under the Derby Borough Education Authority with Mr Smithard as Director."

Mr K.C.Saunders recalls that he attended the school from 1934: "I remember that Mrs Freeman was the headmistress in my day. (*Mrs Freeman was headmistress from 1934-1944.*) "I remember my first day at the Infant School. This was the wooden building in the corner of the playground. The teacher was a Miss Pickerill and she had to chase me round the playground as I did not want to start school!

"Mr Oldham was the headmaster at the Junior School and some teachers I remember are Mr Warden, Mr Ford and Mr Freckleton, the music teacher. At one time we were at the house at the top of Browning

Street, which is now part of Homelands, I believe. I recall playing marbles there! I can also recall an outing, about 1938, to the Manchester Ship Canal. We did a cruise of the whole length of the canal, but I cannot remember which way!"

Normanton Schools — with the infants in the 'West Wing' and the juniors and secondary in the brick building — were all-age schools until the beginning of the 1940s.

Mrs Peggy Westridge recalled that she was on Mrs Freeman's staff for one term,— then with Miss Glover until 1945. Miss Glover was headmistress from 1944 to 1961. "I remember when Miss Glover's smiling face first appeared in the playground, the children rushed to hold her hand or clutch her skirt, they seemed to realise immediately, without a word spoken, that she loved them all."

After World War Two, various changes were made both on the site and in the organisation of the schoool. A kitchen was erected and dinners for children at schools throughout the town of Derby were exported from it. Towards the end of the decade plans were made to build a new Junior School on a site in Grange Avenue, thereby releasing more space to the expanding Infant School.

During the time that Miss B.V.Tindale was the headteacher (1961-1979), the number of pupils was continually increasing.

It became very apparent that a new building was needed. A site for a replacement school was found on allotments off Blackmore Street and construction went ahead. The first classes — the oldest children from the Browning Street School — moved in November 1972. Later, the original building became the annexe to the new school and in 1972-73, the number of pupils there was 84. The headteacher was in one building and the deputy was based at the other, about a mile away. The Blackmore Street building

Normanton School pictured in 1992.

was officially opened on 7 December 1973.

During 1974, re-organisation of local government took place and education in Derby became the responsibility of the Derbyshire County Council.

The policy of the new authority was towards the education of pre-school children, particularly in urban areas, and a nursery was added on to the Blackmore Street School, as an extra building in May 1976.

At the same time, a problem which had to be surmounted was the fact that there were still outdoor toilets at the school in Browning Street. There were also other difficulties associated with this building which was now approaching its Centenary.

In April 1980, under the headship of Elizabeth Lingard — later Mrs Duffy — a thanksgiving service in celebration of the Centenary took place at St Giles' Church which was attended by many old pupils and members of staff as well as leading local educationalists. A party was given for the present pupils and later in the summer term outdoor celebrations continued with the maypole dancing — a long-standing tradition.

By 1984, the number of children on the roll of the Normanton Infant School (both sites) was 320 — it was the largest Infant School in Derbyshire and the only split-site Infant School in the East Midlands. There were six classes based at Browning Street and the school was not viable to operate.

To replace the Browning Street School, the local authority had set aside some land at the bottom of Littleover Lane near the junction of Brayfield Road and Valley Road. It was proposed to build a large primary school with places for 240 infants. Normanton Junior School was to be unaffected by this project. There was much opposition to this idea and as a result upgrading of the Browning Street premises took place in 1983, which included the clearing of the roof space of pigeon droppings, installation of new floors and the lowering of the ceilings.

As far as the 'West Wing' was concerned, a section had been lost in a fire and the rest was demolished in 1985.

Normanton Village Infant School, Browning Street
The split of the Normanton Infant School took place in September 1985. The Blackmore Street School retained the name Normanton Infant School and the school in Browning Street took the name of Normanton Village Infant School.

Days before the former kitchen building was due to be demolished, a decision to use the building as a nursery was made. The idea to establish a nursery at this 'new' school had first been mooted in 1987 and in June 1988, a 26-place nursery was opened to serve the youngsters of the school's catchment area.

Now the school consisted of four classrooms and accommodation was becoming stretched due to increasing numbers. During the summer term it was necessary to use the hall as a classroom. In March 1990, one of the infant classes moved into a terrapin building — with the senior students next door. Unfortunately, during the Spring Bank Holiday there was a fire in these buildings but the infant room was saved.

However, plans went ahead for an extension to the existing building and additional facilities were provided for the children and the staff. The official opening of these rooms was performed in 1991 by John Keith, the Mayor of Derby and a former pupil and governor.

A cherised possession, now taking pride of place in the school hall, and part of the school logo, is the bell which originally summoned children to school from its bell turret above the former main entrance.

Normanton Junior School

As mentioned earlier, Normanton Junior School existed as a combined unit with the Infant School under the headships of Mr Powell and later Mr Oldham.

In 1947, Mr Cresswell was appointed headmaster of the school which was operating from the brick building in Browning Street. However, with the increase in numbers of children which took place following the end of World War Two, the Derby Borough Education Committee began to look for a suitable site for a new school.

A seven-acre site on Grange Avenue was found and planning of the school went ahead. To serve the needs of the community — a clinic was to be built across the road.

The foundation stone of Normanton Junior School was laid by Alderman Matt Lowe, the Mayor of Derby and a local resident, on 14 September 1950. In his remarks during the ceremony, Alderman Lowe stated that he had been involved in the parish discussions in 1928 'when we were faced with the question of whether we should accept an invitation from the County Borough to become part and parcel of the Borough'. He continued: "I held the view then, and I am still firmly convinced, that it was in the interests of Normanton population to join forces with the County Borough."

The building of the school progressed during the following 12 months and the initial phase was ready for the first pupils early in the autumn term of 1951.

The design of the building was carried out by the Borough Architect and the construction was by Ford & Weston Ltd of Osmaston Road, Derby. Building was by means of the 'Orlit' prefabricated system, comprising reinforced concrete posts and beams with concrete slab wall cladding.

The school — planned to accommodate 480 pupils — comprises a kitchen and dining room and was to be equipped with the latest equipment, for example, cinema, radio and epidiascope projection in the classrooms and assembly hall.

A feature of the landscaping of the grounds at the school are the slabs which cover the soil on the banks around the buildings. John Keith recalls: "I think I was in the second class to go to the Junior School. They'd got these slab banks there and the rules were you'd not to go up the banks. You had to stay on the playground. We had two separate playgrounds — one for girls and one for boys. I think a lot used

to get the cane for running up the bank. I became a monitor there in the fourth year. It was a nice school with it being new. In the summer they used to be able to open the doors that lead out on to the balcony that overlooked the fields — this was nice."

To soften the severity of the new buildings and the surroundings, the Parent-Teachers Association donated many of the trees that grace the area today.

Developments in Secondary Education in Normanton

Secondary education — within a separate school — did not come to Normanton until 1938. When the school leaving age was raised to 11 in 1893 and 12 in 1899, the pupils continued to be educated in the brick building in what was then Cabbage Square.

When the leaving age was put up to 14 by the Education Act of 1918, it is assumed that pupils were still being taught in the Normanton Council School, especially in view of the large numbers which Mr Oldham mentions in 1925.

By the early 1930s, Derby had two secondary schools for boys and one for girls. However, central schools were still in existence and girls from the area were attending the school in Hastings Street or the Parkfields School.

Derby Borough Education Committee acquired the estate of the late Giles Austin around this time and set about making plans for the use of the land. An announcement was made on 25 January 1936 to the effect that the 'Education Committee's building programme provides for a new secondary school for girls at Normanton.'
Derby Evening Telegraph, 25 January 1936.

Homelands Secondary School for Girls, later Homelands Grammar School, Village Street.

A report in the *Derbyhsire Advertiser* of 25 June 1937 said: 'The foundation stone of Derby's new secondary school for girls was laid by the Mayor of Derby, Councillor Mrs E.Petty, on 23 June 1937 and marked an important stage in Derby's educational development. The school, which will be known as "Homelands", is estimated to cost £45,750 to provide ten classrooms including a geography room for 30 pupils in each and three classrooms for 20 pupils in each.

"Speaking to the girls, Alderman Dr H.H.Bemrose, Chairman of the Ceremony, said it was, he believed, the first time in Derby that the whole of the girls from the Central School had been present at the laying of a foundation stone. It was the foundation stone of a school to which they would migrate in a few years and they would then not enter a central school but a secondary school, one which would provide further educational facilities. They would be trained for work, for leisure and for responsibility."

The Mayor laid the foundation stone and the Rev R.G.McAlpine (Vicar of St Giles') said the dedication prayer.

Mrs Petty 'went on to speak of the wonderful view those at the school would have across the Vale of Trent. Such a glorious vista would inspire them all

The Village Community School, formerly Homelands Grammar School for Girls, in Village Street.

the time they were at work. The Mayor concluded by wishing true success to the school and its future and to the staff that would be working there.'

The opening ceremony of the new school was performed in September, 1938 by Miss Margaret Keay, MBE, formerly a head at Abbey Street Central School and the first head of Parkfields School.

The school was designed by Mr C.H.Aslin, Borough Architect, and it was reported that 'his vision was of a school amongst the trees and that is a good description of Homelands as we have it today.'
Derbyshire Advertiser, 16 September 1938.

Mr Aslin, commenting on the school 'explained that the entrance to the school faced north and the assembly hall opened directly upon the entrance hall. There were 13 classrooms, two chemistry laboratories, physics and biology laboratories, lecture room, library, geography room, needlework room and an art room. There was a gymnasium with shower baths and changing rooms, headmistress' room and staff rooms. The school was connected to a domestic science block by a covered way and a dining room was provided in this block.'

There were two quadrangles, Mr Aslin added, 'not at their best as yet but designed to add to the amenities of the school'. They would, he thought, 'be found very pleasant'. The whole of the classrooms were on

the south side of the school and looked over the Vale of Trent to Breedon-on-the-Hill. The assembly hall had a fully equipped stage, with head lights, foot lights, etc. The school would accommodate 490 children. The sum of £2,850 had been spent on the furniture, all of which, with the exception of the chairs, had been specially designed.

The initial intake of pupils on 14 September 1938 was 380 — with 19 members of staff. By the time of the 'coming of age' of the school, in September 1959, there were 608 pupils, 29 full-time members of staff and three part-time members. By this time, too, some additions had been made to the original buildings and new laboratories were badly needed.

To commemorate the occasion each form in the school was to provide a tree for planting in the school grounds — 21 of them altogether. However, due to the dry summer of that year, only three trees were planted at a token ceremony. The first tree was planted by Alderman A.Sturgess, chairman of the school governors and present at the laying of the foundation stone. The Director of Education, Mr Charles Middleton, planted the second tree and the third tree was planted jointly by Celia Winterton and Margaret Parker, previous and present head girls.

A service of thanksgiving was held in the Cathedral in mid-September and attended by the present pupils, staff, parents and others associated with the school over the first 21 years.

By now pupils were being educated up to the age of 18 years of age, or to 16 if they wished.

In the corner of the playing fields, close to Kitchener Avenue, a temporary building was erected during World War Two to accommodate a day nursery. Use of the building continued until it was finally demolished in the 1970s.

Normanton Secondary School, Village Street

An event which celebrated the Centenary of the 1870 Education Act was the official opening on 21 September 1970, of Normanton Secondary School. This school, initially with an entrance off Arleston Street, was constructed alongside the Homelands building so as to replace the Old Pear Tree Boys' and Girls' Schools in Harrington and Portland Streets. This school was one of the first six buildings in the County over three storeys high and designed in the CLASP system — a construction technique developed in Nottinghamshire and Derbyshire. This system reduced the time taken in design and construction.

The site available for building was extremely limited and it was felt that the fine views from the site should not be obscured and also that existing trees should be preserved but leaving as much room as possible for playing field purposes. The principal teaching spaces were to be accommodated in a four-storey tower block. The value of Phase I of the work was £242,000 with an additional £17,500 being added for Phase II which consisted of further accommodation. Between 580 and 600 students were to be taught.

A feature on the outside of the building near the main entrance which was designed by Mr J.T.Glover, the art master of the school, is a mural in concrete.

Homelands Comprehensive School

By 1972, comprehensive education was introduced to Derby, and Homelands Grammar School and Normanton Secondary School merged to create the larger Homelands Comprehensive, which, of course, became co-educational at the same time. An opportunity was also taken to re-organise the catchment areas of the schools in the town. A segment starting from the centre of town and spreading out towards the boundary of the Borough was to be the new catchment of Homelands — necessitating a fairly long journey to school for some pupils.

Regrettably, the first half of the 1980s was marred by damage by fire, arson attacks and the discovery of asbestos in the buildings.

Village Community School

By September 1989, the County Education Committee had decided to reorganise secondary education in the city and to create sixth-form colleges. Therefore, teaching at the schools was to be up to the age of 16 years with any further tuition being continued in one of the two further education colleges in the city.

The opportunity was taken at this time to change the name of Homelands Comprehensive School to the Village Community School.

Farms and Houses and Rose Cottage

TODAY the only reminders of the many farms which once flourished in Normanton are the old house at 185 Village Street, near the corner of Browning Street, now a Grade II listed building, which was part of Edge's Old Hall Farm, and another house end-on to Village Street, opposite Chatham Street, which was the farmhouse of Rosedale Farm. In addition, part of the old Cottons farmhouse at Sinfin still survives.

Little is known of the farms which have gone, but Booth's Red Thorn Farm was opposite the church where the council houses are, and the site of Hallsworth's Rose Farm with the bakery on the corner of Village Street and Derby Lane is now occupied by the Greyhound Hotel.

Where the Sherwood Forester Hotel now stands there was a rambling farmhouse. Wallbrooks Farm was at the bottom of Derby Lane, and there were also farms on Sunny Hill.

Old Hall Farm

Mr Joe Harrison, when recalling memories of his time at the village school in the early part of this century, said: "Edge's Farm across the road could always provide some interest, for the cows came down the lane most days to be milked, midsummer saw haymaking time, and a little later it was the turn of the corn to be brought home. About October a huge traction and threshing machine came to thresh the corn and provide a loud humming background to our lessons."

In an account of an interview with Mr William Edge of Old Hall Farm which appeared in the *Derby Evening Telegraph* in 1951, he said he believed the farm to have been in his family's possession for many generations. The writer, Stuart Wilkinson, went on:

"Mr Edge is one of those men for whom it is impossible not to feel respect at first sight. Find him in the yard of his farm, as I did, and his personality meets you before you can get near enough for a formal handshake.

"I had the feeling that if Mr Edge was unimpressed by a visitor, that person would find himself not merely unwelcome, but very soon off the premises.

"The heavily-studded door of the farmhouse itself is thought to have come from the old Normanton Hall and Mr Edge has maintained the air of antiquity in the house by refusing to make use of gas or electricity. Instead, he employs an old-fashioned kitchen range and, when the sun's rays fade from his

Rear view of Old Hall Farm.

Mr Edge admiring one of his exotic plants.

Winter view at the back of Old Hall Farm.

world of enviable tranquility, paraffin lamps are lighted.

"It stands only a stone's throw from bustling streets, yet it is in what Mr Edge calls his 'homestead' — a magnificent garden at the rear of his Village Street home — that there is all the colour and peace of the heart of the country. On the walls of the garden and some of the outbuildings are perfectly trained fruit trees which have taken years to shape — in one case 35 years. The clinging branches of this huge pear tree follow unerringly the lines of the bricks of the wall — straight as the back of the man in the weather-

Studded door and well at Old Hall Farm.

beaten straw hat who trained them.

"But the fruit trees . . .are only a part of the interest of the 'homestead'. Here, culled from the four corners of the earth, are shrubs in astounding variety — a display rivalling any outside Kew Gardens. Many of them stand in the soil of their native lands — Chile and China among them — which was imported to maintain their existence.

"For quite a long time Mr Edge showed me round this 'international paradise' pointing out with pride the peculiarities of each shrub — the 'Peacock' that took 35 years to train and the 'Teddy-bear' that took 25.

'Although he still owns many acres of farmland, he has lost a great deal by way of compulsory purchase — in the interest of building, but the pride of his forebears in the land that yielded their livelihood is reflected in the sparkling eyes of Mr Edge."

The property passed out of the ownership of the Edge family some years ago.

Sinfin Lane Farm

An intriguing story about an ancient gold ring being found on the property known as Sinfin Lane Farm, owned by Mr William Gray, is recorded in the *Journal of the Derby Archaeological and Natural History Society* for 1885 as follows:

"In September 1883, Mr Gray was proposing to enlarge some outbuildings in the field at the back of his house. In removing the soil, at a depth of about 18 inches, the workman's pick struck and turned up the ring, thus bringing to light a most valuable and interesting relic of the past. The ring lay perfectly loose in the soil; there were no old stones, nor foundations of any kind, no pottery, metal, nor bones near where it was found: in fact there would seem to be absolutely no explanation of the presence of the ring in that particular spot. The only discernible peculiarity of the find was that the soil in which the ring lay, for about a square yard round, was of dark coloured earth, whereas the soil of the field is common yellow clay.

"The ring itself is of the purest gold, the

Lake House stables.

workmanship very rude, the design — a roughly twisted cable widening into a flat round signet. The contrast, however, between the careless general design, and the engraving of the signet, is most marked. Nothing could be more exquisitely finished than the sharp details of the engraving...The device represents St Michael, with shield and spear, trampling and transfixing the dragon, the minutest details of features, feathers or scales, being carved with a woundrous care and skill.

"It was suggested by experts that the ring was a religious or ecclesiastical ring probably made in the fourteenth century, and the author of the article comments 'How a ring made for ecclesiastical use in the reign, probably, of Edward III came to be lost in a field at Normanton-by-Derby it is useless to speculate . . .' Sadly this is where the story seems to end for there is no known record of where the ring is today."

Houses

Lake House, once a farm, which stood on land at the corner of Derby Lane and Village Street, was demolished in 1936 and Lake Drive marks where it stood. The site was shown as a freehold property with house on the 1605 map but the first mention of it by name appears to be in a marriage settlement of 1724 when the owner was Michael Willson 'yeoman of Normanton'. In 1840 the Lake House property was purchased from the Willsons by Mr Goodale, whose family owned a lead works and tannery off Normanton Road which later became Offiler's brewery. The Goodales acquired considerable land and property in Normanton, including Normanton House. The last occupant of Lake House was Mr Frederick Fletcher,

lace manufacturer, and the house stood empty for some time before it was demolished.

Normanton House in Village Street, understood to be the oldest house in Normanton, is now part of the Village Community School. It was built in 1740 by the Dixies who were connected to the Beaumont family by marriage. It became the property of the Goodales c.1819 and later was lived in by Mr Richard Sale and then Mr Willn before the house and estate were purchased by Mr John Shaw in the early 1870s. In the entrance hall the frieze decorated with sheep may be an indication that at one time the owners were farmers.

Over the years the beautifully laid out grounds of Normanton House were used for fêtes, bazaars and sales of work in aid of various causes such as the Church Rebuilding Fund, the School Fund and the Clothing Club. People from outside the village were obviously attracted to these events — on one such occasion, in 1878, the local Press advertised that omnibuses (horse-drawn at that time) would be run every hour from the Royal Hotel in Derby to Normanton House, for a forthcoming sale of work at which the Band of the 1st Derby Militia would be playing.

When the estate was purchased by Mr Giles Austin, after Mr Shaw's death in 1906, he built himself a new house, Homelands House, in the grounds, and Normanton House was occupied by tenants. Following Mr Austin's death in 1929, Derby Corporation acquired the estate, and Homelands Grammar School for Girls (now Village Community School) was built on land fronting Village Street in 1937.

Normanton House was occupied by Army person-

Normanton House, photographed by Keene after 1901.

Part of Normanton House pictured in July 1992. Note the detail on the surrounds to the porch.

nel during World War Two. From 1948-1971 it was used as a Course Centre for the National Nursery Examination Board and after this as the Sixth Form block for Homelands School. Since 1992 it has been used by the Community Education Council. The village lost another link with the past when the old stables and coachhouse on Village Street were demolished in 1988. Applications for Normanton House to be registered as a listed building have been refused on the grounds of the extent of the alterations to the original building which have taken place. It is reassuring that essential repairs and remedial work have now been put in hand.

Miss Mary Shaw, who died early in 1993 aged 90 and was the granddaughter of Mr John Shaw, had memories of staying at Normanton House with her mother for a funeral, when she was very young, and remembered the roaring fires in the grates.

In the 1800s, **Park Hill**, at the top of Browning Street, was the home of Mr Robert Radford who spent his early years at Cottons Farm. After retiring as tenant of one of the largest farms on the Aston estate he came to Normanton where he purchased an estate and farmed 40 acres. Park Hill was last lived in as a private house by Mr Ernest Grimes and his family. He owned a drapery business near The Spot in Derby, which closed in 1955. The property has, for many years, been used as a social club by the International Combustion Company.

Homelands House, Old Normanton.

Evington House, Old Normanton.

Fern Cottage at the north-west corner of the crossroads, opposite Evington House. Note the signpost.

The Grange, probably built between 1865-70, was approached by a tree-lined drive (now Ingleby Avenue) from Village Street. The lodge still stands but the stables went when No 211 Village Street was built. It was the home of Mr Charles Brentnall, maltster and farmer, until his death in 1886. Later owners were Mr T.G.Clayton, manager of the Midland Railway Carriage & Wagon Works, and Capt M.L.Paget. It became a public house in 1932.

Evington House, facing Littleover Lane at the corner of Village Street and Stenson Road, was built about the same time as The Grange and one of the early owners was Mr W.Briggs, Solicitor. During World War One it was used as an auxiliary hospital. It was converted to a social club in the 1920s. Vine Cottage on Stenson Road was the gardener's cottage.

The Knoll, on the opposite corner of Village Street and Stenson Road, first mentioned c.1888, was the home Mr Edward Brentnall, paper bag manufacturer, who was the youngest son of Mr Charles Brentnall of The Grange. Later owners included Mr Albert Green, JP, and Mr Francis Powell, solicitor, whose widow was the last to live there before it was demolished and a purpose built home for the handicapped built on the site.

Continuing down Stenson Road towards Sunny-hill, the next house was **Normanton Lodge** — in the 1920s the home of Alderman William Hart, JP, a Freeman of Derby. It, too, was eventually demolished and sheltered housing for the elderly built on the site in 1977.

Next to this was **Holmfield,** built in the 1890s, and lived in c.1895 by Mr W.T.M.Orme, and c.1922 by

Cottages, now demolished, on the north side of Village Street.

Rose Cottage, Village Street, pictured in 1983.

Mr John James Doughty JP. Mr Arthur Holmes, a builder and son of the founder of the firm (Arthur Holmes and Sons) bought the property towards the end of World War Two and lived there until the 1980s. It was subsequently pulled down and flats for older people built there.

Mr Sidney Porter, who was a well-known Derby businessman, lived at the next house down, **White Gates.** He had an aviary in the garden and sometimes parrots could be glimpsed in the trees. The house has now been suitably altered and extended to become the Littleover Nursing Home.

A large house, **The Mount,** set in spacious grounds, stood well back from Stenson Road in the area where Ainsworth, Walton, Masefield and Gaskell Avenues now stand. It was the home of Mr Archibald Laing (pronounced Lane), manager of the Derby branch of the London and Midland Bank, who died in 1892 and the family remained the owners until the land was redeveloped.

Few cottages remain in Village Street apart from those between the corner of Browning Street and St Giles' Church, and **Rose Cottage** near Newlyn Drive.

It is understood that another cottage once stood in front of Rose Cottage with a 'nursery rhyme' well in the front garden.

Now Rose Cottage is the home of Mrs Margaret Beckett, MP Deputy Leader of the Labour Party, and her husband, Leo. When she won Derby South in 1983, they looked for a house in the constituency and found the 150-year-old cottage in Normanton, with oak beams and roses round the door, just what they wanted.

The Radfords of Normanton-by-Derby

IN 1750 the village did not exceed 30 houses and following the Enclosure Act of 1768, a map of the Lordship of Normanton c.1769 from a map of 1728 by John Grundy, shows many closes and pingles with several new names as proprietors. These included Robert Goodale, John Wilson, Lord Huntingdon, Samuel Crompton and Repton School (writes Peter H.Thompson).

The largest tenanted farm was The Cottons Farm which extended from the old Barracks to Sinfin Moor, in area about 380 acres. It was farmed until about 1894 by the Radford family whose name appears in the Normanton registers in the mid-1700s.

My great-great-great-grandfather John Radford, born 1759, was a yeoman farmer in Normanton until his death on 8 May 1833, aged 74. His house and homestead were on Village Street, with a parcel of land called the Rickyard adjoining, a cowhouse, stable and garden. In 1788 he married Mary Gibson, daughter of John Gibson and Mary (née Harrison) of Mickleover at Derby St Peter's. In his will he left various parcels of land, closes, livestock, personal goods, 'my house and homestead in Normanton in which I now reside', to his youngest son Richard, with legacies to other sons and daughters. Various closes are named and can be identified on old maps, eg the Two Far Marsh Closes and the Marsh Close adjoining or near to Sadler's Flatt, the Two Near Marsh Closes and Far Slade Marsh Close. It is interesting to note the number of closes, following the Enclosure Act. It seems that the 'House and Homestead' existed on Village Street on the site of the later Old Hall Farm which belonged to the Edge family with whom members of the Radford family inter-married. The Old Hall Farmhouse still stands on Village Street today.

Richard Radford, John's youngest son, who inherited the farm, married Hannah Land of Normanton at Derby St Peter's on 24 January 1825 and later moved to Walnut House, Stenson. According to the 1861 census he was farming 270 acres, employing three men and one boy. Richard, who died on 29 September 1871, and Hannah are buried in Normanton Churchyard. Their epitaph reads: 'There the wicked cease from troubling and there the weary get rest. Job 3:17'

Other children of John and Mary Radford include: Mary, wife of John Wilson; Joseph, a publican of Turnditch; William, a butcher of the Normanton Road; Dorothy, the wife of William Johnson, publican of Hopping Hill and Ann, my great-great-grandmother who married George Pemberton,

builder. Surprisingly, one of his oldest sons, Robert, born 1796, who farmed the Cottons Farm was not mentioned in his father's will. John, who died in 1833, is also buried in Normanton Churchyard. His epitaph reads:

'John Radford — Who departed this life
May 8 1833 aged 74 years.
'In Christ he died — what can words express
'To make the sorrow of the mourners less
'The God he served is now his joy
'And songs of praise his Powers employ.'

Meanwhile, Robert was farming 160 acres of The Cottons Farm according to the 1851 census. He had married Ann Stevenson, daughter of Thomas Stevenson of Snareston in 1822. The 1851 census lists five children, the eldest being Robert junior born 1823 and a servant, Jane Brownsword — a well-known Normanton name. The 1861 census shows that Robert had increased his land to 270 acres and upon his death at the Cottons House in 1872, his youngest son, Edwin, inherited the Cottons Farm, now increased to 285 acres and employing six men and two boys plus a dairymaid and two servants.

This branch of the Radfords farmed the Cottons Farm until 1893-94, when Edwin purchased the Haynford Lodge Estate in Norfolk and the whole farm, livestock etc., was transported by rail, 'lock stock and barrel'. Edwin, born 1840, had married Georgina Edge and it is believed that the move to Norfolk was partly for health reasons and partly because of the impending expansion of Derby into its surrounding countryside.

A transcript taken from a copy of 'The Journal' in the *Norwich Mercury* dated Saturday, 11 August 1928 reads as follows:

'Late Mr E.Radford
Death of Haynford's public benefactor.
The death occurred at Haynford Lodge on Thursday (2 August 1928) of Mr Edwin Radford, an octogenarian farmer and landowner, well-known and highly respected in this part of the county. He was born at Normanton, near Derby, in 1840. In 1875 he married Miss Georgina Edge, who, having pre-deceased him, he married in 1903, Mrs C.Cousins, of Terrington. Mr Radford farmed extensively in Derbyshire and later at Frettenham and Haynford, and became a well-known figure at Norwich Corn Hall and Cattle Market. Mr Radford's activities were not limited to his business as an agriculturist. For a number of years he was a member of St Faith's Rural District Council. Always showing a keen interest in church and parochial matters, for over 30 years he held office

Mrs Sarah Riley (neé Radford) dressed to attend Mr (later Lord) Winterbottom's Hunt Ball at Aston Hall, c.1891. Mr Winterbottom purchased some jewellery for her to wear, and keep, if she would act as his hostess due to his wife's illness. The jewellery is now in the possession of Miss Nancy Radford.

as Church Warden at Haynford as well as at Normanton (Derbyshire), while as School Manager at Haynford he interested himself in the educational side of village life. As recently as last year he gave Haynford their playing field as well as additional land on which to build a Parish Hall. His death is a great loss to the Parish. Mr Radford leaves four sons, all noted farmers.'

In 1895, Cottons Farm was being farmed by Frederick Johnson, according to *Kelly's Directory* of 1895, which also lists the principal landowners of Normanton as John Shaw Esq of Normanton House, Mr Goodale, Messrs Robert, Richard and Edwin Radford, Messrs Reginald and Raymond Roumieu and Lt-Col George Newdigate. A brief summary stated that 'the soil is loam; subsoil clay and marl, mostly pasture; corn is grown to a very small extent. The area is 1,180 acres; rateable value £10,178'.

In 1891 the population of Normanton was 1,186 and of those 248 resided at the Barracks. By the Derby Corporation Act 1890, that part of Normanton included in the municipal borough was created a separate parish, designated New Normanton and is given with the Borough of Derby.

In 1921, Cottons Farm was purchased by Derby Borough Council from Arthur Jessop, a wool merchant from York, and the golf-course was laid out in 1924. A further portion of land was allocated to build the houses in Thackeray Street in 1931-32 and another small piece to build Moorside Crescent in 1977.

In 1922, the engineering company International Combustion Ltd acquired 55 acres of land fronting Sinfin Lane (formerly Cotton Lane) and the old firm W. & J.Richardson (established 1624), tanners, curriers and belting manufacturers, established their Eagle Leather Works on the site of the Old Brickworks. Here was a very deep pond, formed by excavating the clay for bricks for the Normanton Barracks, which was well stocked with perch around which fishermen would spend many happy hours. Water from the pond was pumped to a storage tank inside their works and many a perch was taken from this tank. It was said that a horse and cart toppled into this 'bottomless' pond, never to be seen again!

Cottons is an ancient name. The 1605 map of the Manor of Normanton shows many areas thus designated *eg* Middle Cotton, Far Cotton, Rough Cotton etc., and the old road (Cotton Lane) ran from Osmaston Road along the present Cotton Lane, Elton Road, Osmaston Park Road and down Sinfin Lane, all formerly Cotton Lane. The site of Cottons Farm is an ancient settlement. Notice the reference in *The Domesday Book, England's Heritage, Then and Now* edited by Thomas Hinde: 'Cottons; Codetune: Kings Land, Henry de Ferrers. Cottons Farm.' The present Cottons Farm probably dates from the late 1700s and the variety of brick bonds suggest additions at different periods. It was the largest farm extending from the former Normanton Barracks to Sinfin Moor, in area about 380 acres.

Robert Radford, who died at the Cottons House in 1872, had other lands which are mentioned in his will proved at Derby on 15th February 1873. These included 'two closes of land called the Hall on Hell Meadows, situated in the Parish of Littleover, two closes of land called The Long House and Top Heanor situated partly in the Township of Normanton and partly in the Parish of Littleover, a close of land called Sunny Hill situated in the Parish of Littleover, a close of land called The Top Marsh situated in the Township of Normanton'.

In addition he left his messuage, cottages, lands and hereditaments situate in the Parish of Alvaston in the County of Derby, to his son Joseph Radford and it is interesting to note that there is a Radford Street in Alvaston.

Robert's eldest son, also Robert, who spent his early life at Cottons Farm, married Ann Buck Newton in 1850. She was a member of another old Derbyshire family and reputed to be a descendant of Sir Isaac Newton. A brief summary of this Robert is found in his obituary in the *Derby Mercury*, 27 March 1908 under the heading 'The Late Mr Robert Radford — A Derbyshire Yeoman' which reads as follows: 'At Normanton-by-Derby on Monday, the funeral took place of Mr Robert Radford who for many years was one of the most prominent farmers in the district of Derby. A descendant of a well-known yeoman family, the deceased spent his early life at the Cottons Farm, Normanton-by-Derby and when 27 years of age he married Ann Buck Newton, a member of another old family. In 1850 he became the tenant of the largest farm on the Aston Estate, under Squire Holden and during the many years he remained there he was one of the leading men in the village, filling all the important parish offices. He was also churchwarden and rendered invaluable service in many other ways. In farming he displayed great ability and he was the winner of many prizes, including a cup given in an open county competition for the best managed farm. The adjudicators at the time stated that they had never seen a farm so excellently stocked or better managed.

'Mr Radford resided at Aston for 29 years and when he retired into private life he went into residence at Normanton-by-Derby, where he purchased an estate (Park Hill) and continued to farm some 40 acres of land.

'Mr Radford sat on the Board of Guardians for the Shardlow Union, was a member of the Old Normanton School Board, and was one of the original members of the Parish Council. His advice was largely sought-after and never refused. He was one of the best judges of stock and for many years was a regular attendant at Derby Market. A man of kind heart and genial temperament, his purse was ever accessible for charitable and philanthropic objects.

'The burial service was impressively read by the Vicar, the Revd J.Glass, assisted by the Rector of Aston, the Rev J.S.Holden. The coffin was of polished English oak with brass appointments and shield engraved 'Robert Radford. Died March 19 1908, aged 84 years'.

'The mourners were: Mr T.Turner, Mrs Turner,

Mr and Mrs Riley, Mr and Mrs Dudeney, Mr R.Radford, Mrs Burton, Mr R.Jerram, Mrs Tabberer, Mr C.Kirk and Mr R.Wood.

'There were also present: Alderman W.Hart, Dr Reid and Mr W.Powell. The selected pall bearers were: Mr Robert Turner, Mr O.Vickers, Mr P.Riley, Mr A.Burton, Mr T.Turner and Mr W.Riley. The funeral arrangements were in the hands of Thomas Lloyd and Co Limited, Derby'.

Ann Buck Radford died at Park Hill in 1882, aged 62, and after Robert's death in 1908 the house was subsequently owned by the Grimes family — well-known drapers in Derby — of whom Commander R.C.D.Grimes was Conservative candidate for Derby South in the 1950s.

Park Hill was purchased by Messrs International Combustion Ltd in 1949 from the Grimes family for £3,000 and part of it used initially as a drawing office. In 1953 planning permission was obtained for use as a social club and a conference/concert hall was built on. A bowling green was laid out in front of the house. This is the present role of Park Hill.

There is a stained glass window in St Giles' Church, Normanton-by-Derby, inscribed: 'To the glory of the Lord and in loving memory of Ann Buck, wife of Robert Radford, Park Hill, Normanton, born 24 February 1820.' A plaque alongside says, 'This window was placed in the church to the glory of God and in memory of Ann Buck Radford who died 12 May 1882, aged 62 years, by her children.'

A plaque over the reredos says: 'This reredos was erected to the glory of God and in memory of Robert Radford, who died 19 March 1908, aged 84 years, by his children.'

In addition there are several Radford graves with memorial inscriptions in Normanton Churchyard.

Robert's brother John, born 1829, of Mount Villa, Village Street, Normanton, was also a farmer and in his will, proved in 1908, he left to his son John (born 1865) 'a clear legacy of £300 with all my furniture, linen, china, books, pictures, wearing apparel, ornaments, wine and other liquors, horses, carriages and all other effects in and about my house and all live and dead farming stock, implements, stores and ancilliary effects, house, gardens etc'.

His son John, who described himself as a 'gentleman', also of Mount Villa, died in 1914 leaving his estate to his wife Edith Sarah Radford.

Old Normanton still retains a little of its rural atmosphere, its church and churchyard, Normanton House and several other great houses, although with modified uses. There are still far reaching views across the Trent Valley to Breedon and beyond from various vantage points, notably Park Hill. Finally, there continues to be a link with the past in Cottons Farm which is still being farmed today, although on a much smaller scale.

Derby Mayors From Normanton

NORMANTON has provided several elected members to the Borough and later the City Council, who have become Mayors. An interesting factor, too, is that a handful lived in, or had connections with, the same road — Stenson Road.

Alderman William Hart JP

Born: 22 January 1858; Died: 30 October 1929. Residence: Normanton Lodge, Stenson Road, Derby. William Hart was born in Nottingham but spent most of his life in Derby. He began his career working in the office of the Borough Accountant, where he gained detailed knowledge of financial matters. Mr Hart also became familiar with Registration Law and in 1885 he became an election agent.

Also in 1885, he began his own business as an accountant and ten years later relinquished the political agency.

Mr Hart was a former auditor of the Derby Savings Bank and Derby and Derbyshire Permanent Building Society. He was a director of Offilers' Brewery Ltd, the Derby Coal Company and the Derby Gas Company amongst others. He was also a County and Borough Magistrate.

He married a Miss Jerram, who was a member of a family long associated with the agricultural industry of Etwall.

In 1889, William Hart was elected a member of the Town Council representing Babington Ward. However, in 1901, upon the extension of the Borough, he was allocated to the new division of Dale Ward which he continued to represent until his elevation to the aldermanic bench in 1905.

'In his work he combined a ready ability with vigour and energy, and was certainly one of the most practical men in the council.' *Modern Mayors of Derby.*

The Mayoralty of Mr Hart commenced on 9 November 1904 — a period of steady and useful work. During his year the electric tramways to New Normanton and Pear Tree were connected into a circular route and the Kedleston Road route was put in place.

Due largely to Alderman Hart's efforts, an invitation was extended to the Royal Agricultural Show to hold their show in Derby in 1906. This was attended by the King.

Miss D. Hart, the Mayor's daughter, had the privilege of presenting a handsome bouquet to Mrs Mundy of Markeaton on 21 June 1905. Mrs Mundy had opened the pleasure ground, which she had given to the town. This was a stretch of land on the opposite side of the road to the Markeaton Recreation Ground — given previously by her husband.

Alderman Hart was a churchwarden at St Giles' in 1908-09, at the time of the memorial service to the 8th Duke of Devonshire who had been Honorary Colonel of the Third Battalion of the Sherwood Foresters, whose Regimental Chapel was at the Parish Church.

Alderman Hart received the Honorary Freedom of the Borough only a month before his death.

His funeral service was held at St Giles' Church — which was filled 'by a large congregation of old friends and former business associates'. The report continued: 'The cortege was led by an escort of uniformed officers and men of the Derby Borough Police from Alderman Hart's home, via Village Street to the church. The path through the churchyard to the church door was lined by the Policemen.' *Derby Daily Express* 4 November 1929.

The service was conducted by the Revd R. Price (the Vicar), the Bishop of Derby and Canon H. Ham. The Bishop, in his address, said that Alderman Hart 'was a man who religiously practised the doctrine of service above self'. *Derby Daily Express*, 4 November 1929. The mourners, led by members of the family, included the Mayor, Councillor J. Ferguson Bell; Captain P. C. Cooper Parry; Mr H. C. Offiler, Dr H. H. Bemrose; Mr J. G. Shields and Mr W. T. Mansfield Orme (who had lived at Holmfield, Stenson Road).

Alderman Hart was buried in the family grave in Nottingham Road Cemetery and as the cortege made its way from the church, Derby people 'along all parts of the route stood with bared and bowed heads in silent respect for a fine municipal leader'. *Derby Daily Express*, 4 November 1929.

Alderman Albert Green JP

Residence: The Knoll, Village Street, Derby.
Alderman Albert Green was born in King Street but his family later moved to Pear Tree Road and he was, therefore, a pupil at St James' Road Council School. After leaving the Technical College, Albert entered his father's business — Messrs Albert Green, Ltd, silk and trimming manufacturers of Agard Street,

Derby, and New Normanton Mills, Charlotte Street, Derby.

When Mr Green joined the firm, 40 hands were employed. He took control in 1902 on the death of his father. Thirteen years later, when he took on the Mayoralty, the firm employed about 1,000 operatives.

Albert Green married Miss Mary Turner of Derby and they had two sons.

He had been a prominent local athlete as a young man, particularly concentrating on cycling. He was a member of the National Cyclists' Union and won numerous prizes and trophies, including a cycling championship of Derbyshire. For 26 years he was President of the Normanton Bowls Club and President of the Derby and County Racing Cyclists Club and of the Derby Amateur Athletics Club.

Councillor Green first entered the Town Council in 1911 as member for Dale Ward — with a majority of four votes.

His first function as Mayor was on 13 November 1915. Five hundred employees were entertained to a tea, concert and dance in the firm's new building in Charlotte Street. During the interval a presentation of a pair of candelabra and a silver rose bowl was made by the work people to honour Councillor Green's elevation to the position of Mayor. Mrs Green received a bonquet of white chrysanthemums from the gimpers.

On the same day in May 1916, the Mayor opened the two Carnegie branch libraries at Alvaston and what is now referred to as 'Pear Tree'.

Lord Kitchener's death took place during this Mayoralty — which was midway through World War One.

On a lighter note, the Mayoress began a series of garden parties at The Knoll during the summer — in aid of local war funds.

In 1917, Mr Green was raised to the aldermanic bench and was Coalition Conservative Member of Parliament for the Borough of Derby from 1918-1922. He belonged to an old Wesleyan family and like his grandfather and father before him was a Freeman of the Borough.

Alderman Green died at The Pastures, Duffield, aged 66 years after three years of poor health. The funeral service was held at Rose Hill Methodist Church, Normanton Road, Derby, and interment was in Sunny Hill Cemetery.

He was succeeded in the business — which now operates from Agard Street only — by his son, Wilfred H.Green.

Alderman 'Matt' Lowe OBE.

Born: 1893; Died: February, 1980. Residences: 116 Stenson Road and Grange Avenue, Normanton.
'Matt' Lowe was born in Rochdale — the youngest of a family of nine. Two years after the trade slump of 1908, at the age of 17, he decided to go to America. He spent four years there, returning to visit his brother who was employed by Rolls-Royce Ltd in Derby. He was advised to obtain employment and to make his

home here — which he did. Later, he met his future wife — Miss Mary Porter — the daughter of Alderman Frank Porter. She was an active worker in the Independent Labour Party.

From 1920, Matt became active in the Trade Union and Political movements and he became a member of County Borough Council in January 1929. He lost his seat for a short period but was returned as representative for Normanton Ward in 1934 — a position he held until being elevated to the aldermanic bench.

In 1930, Mr Lowe became a full-time organiser for the National Union of General and Municipal workers eventually becoming Chief Officer in the East Midlands and Coast District.

The Mayoralty of Alderman Lowe began in May 1950. He was awarded the OBE on 1 January 1968 and this was followed in mid-March by the granting of the Honorary Freedom of the Borough.

His council service ended in 1968 when the entire council was dissolved. Mr Lowe died in February 1980 at the age of 87 years. His funeral took place at Markeaton Crematorium.

Alderman A.H.Slaney JP

Residence: Kenilworth Avenue.
Alderman A.H.Slaney, a native of Derby, was Mayor in 1933-34. For a short while after leaving Traffic Street School he worked as an errand boy but later became an apprentice in the coach building department of the old Midland Railway, where he remained. He saw some of his own handiwork when the Royal Scot train visited Derby after a triumphal tour of North America, and, as Mayor, he opened the first door with a silver key.

He entered the Town Council in 1919 as a Labour member for Arboretum Ward. During his Mayoralty, Mr Slaney opened the first completed part of the nurses' home at the City Hospital, and at the annual Hospital Carnival he 'opened' the new lake in Markeaton Park.

Alderman E.E.Paulson

Residence: 242 Village Street.
Alderman E.E.Paulson was born in Litchurch Ward, which he represented from 1921, and was Mayor in 1937-38. At the age of 11 he started work as a boot boy but three years later he joined the Midland Railway as an apprentice in the locomotive works.

One of the proudest moments of his life was when, during his Mayoralty, he was a guest of the Lord Mayor of London at the Mansion House and rode in a gilded coach attended by liveried footmen. The one-time poor boy from Derby had got somewhere. "I felt like Dick Whittington," he said later. He was Chairman of the Watch Committee for 21 years, longer than any previous holder of the office, and knew practically every police officer in the Borough by name.

Councillor John H.Keith

Born: May 1944. Residence: Bamford Avenue, Normanton.

John Keith was brought up close to Village Street and attended Normanton School, Browning Street — the infants starting in the 'West Wing'. He recalls his first days at school were not happy ones. During his primary years the 'new' Normanton Junior School was opened under the headship of Mr Cresswell and John and his form were the second intake to this school.

Very close to the Keith family's home, severe damage was caused by the bomb that dropped in the area and repairs took a long time to complete. John attended the church Sunday School and was a member of the choir for several years.

Vivid memories of Scouting with the 4th Derby (Derwent) and Captain Bennett are recalled, especially the Bonfire Night celebrations held at the HQ in Coleridge Street.

John attended Pear Tree Boys' School and colleges in Derby and Bolton before beginning work at Rolls-Royce Ltd. Employment with other local and national companies followed before he transferred to the security business. He is now a partner in a security systems company.

He married Susan in June 1969 — shortly after the Revd Barrie Blowers became the incumbent at St Giles'.

The political career of John Keith began when he was elected to represent Normanton on the City Council in 1976. He held this seat for three years and in 1982 was elected to represent the Blagreaves Ward — which he still holds.

His mayoralty began in 1991 and he was dubbed 'Action Man Mayor' because of the activities he involved himself in, for example, abseiling down the nurses' home at the Derbyshire Royal Infirmary in aid of charity; 'flying' over a stage like Peter Pan and driving a JCB in the 'Dancing Diggers Show'. Towards the end of his term of office he greeted the Queen when she arrived to open the Queen's Leisure Centre in Cathedral Road.

Several events connected with Normanton were attended by John Keith during his term of office. He officially opened the new extension to Normanton Village Infant School in 1991. Not only was he a former pupil of the school but also previously chair of the governers. In May 1992, John opened the Normanton Local History Festival, consisting of static exhibits, talks and reminiscences.

John Keith was the second mayor this decade to hold the casting vote in a hung council.

A Thanksgiving Service towards the end of the mayoralty was held in St Giles' Church.

Amongst his hobbies and interests, John counts conjuring — he is a member of the Magic Circle — photography and walking.

Other Political Figures

Another well-known local personality involved in politics was Mr Frank Porter of 149 Stenson Road, Derby. He was born in 1869, in Australia, where his parents had gone to seek their fortune in the Gold Rush. His father found an early grave and Mrs Porter, almost penniless, returned to England with her young family of four sons and two daughters. On arrival in Derby, Frank's intention was to 'make his name'

He began his business at the age of 12 in Liversage Street. He had a horse and dray, and originally the firm were house furnishers and removers. Ultimately, the company developed into one of the largest furniture removal businesses in the Midlands. Into the 1960s, Messrs F.Porter & Son had many large motor vehicles, warehousing and garaging all in the same area where the business first began.

Frank was first elected Labour representative for Castle Ward in 1919. He was a member of the Board of Guardians (which became the Social Welfare Committee), for many years.

He became an Alderman in 1928 and was 'outspoken and imperturbable. He enjoyed his reputation as a rebel, never more so than when religious matters were discussed, for he was a 'Freethinker' with a vengeance. He retained the liveliest admiration for his brother Fred,' despite their political differences. *Derby Evening Telegraph*, 29 October 1951.

In 1933, Mr Porter bought a 45hp saloon car with an enormous bonnet — for £15. Apparently it was finished in burr-walnut, had six large headlights, silk tapestry linings, a luncheon table, cocktail bar and tyres like those of a bus. The car was supposed to have been built in 1926 for the exiled Kaiser — but never delivered. When new, the car had cost £3,000. Its drawbacks were the cost of the tax and its eight miles to each gallon of petrol.

Frank retired from his council work in 1938 because of ill health — the reason he also relinquished his position as head of his firm. He was living in Middleton Avenue, Littleover, when he died in 1947, leaving a widow and two sons and two daughters. His cremation took place at Ruddington in Nottinghamshire.

Other Normanton people involved in political life include David Lightbown, MP for Staffordshire South-East, currently Comptroller of the Household and a Government whip, Councillor Alan Mullarkey of Offerton Avenue and former Councillor John Godfrey, all of whom previously lived in the Offerton Avenue area.

Some Normanton Businesses

W & J Richardson, Eagle Leather Works

ON Sinfin Lane to the south of Normanton Barracks were the Eagle Leather Works and Tannery belonging to W & J Richardson. They were a well-known Derby family. Two played cricket for Derbyshire (one, A.W.Richardson, captaining the county to its only Championship win in 1936) whilst another became Archdeacon of Derby. They trace their original tannery to Horsley Woodhouse, where they were farmers, in 1624.

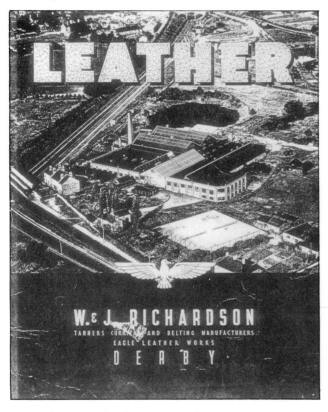

In 1700, the business moved to St Peter's Street, Derby, where it carried out the tanning and also made up leather articles. With the Industrial Revolution, the business prospered and grew, moving to larger premises in Eagle Street in the 1800s.

Following a disastrous fire at the Eagle Street Works in 1929, the business moved to Sinfin Lane — an ideal site with the adjacent railway sidings for the delivery of coal and with an abundant supply of water. However, falling trade brought about its closure in 1984.

Richardsons' concentration on high quality leather called for particular skills and typical examples were leather for both cricket balls and footballs and for the bridle and saddlery trade. Also in years past, miles and miles of belting left Derby to keep the machines of mills and factories turning, but this eventually gave way to a substantial trade in hydraulic seals and packing.

Although leather making is a trade calling for skill, dedication and craftsmanship learned over a thorough apprenticeship, an indenture of 1833 which has been preserved makes strange reading today:

'During which time the said Apprentice his Masters faithfully shall serve, their secrets keep, their lawful commands everywhere glady do . . .he shall not enter into matrimony within the said term . . .nor play at cards or dice . . .shall not haunt taverns or playhouses . . .'

NEI International Combustion Ltd

INTERNATIONAL Combustion has played a part in Britain's engineering industry for over 60 years. Originally established in 1925, today they form one of the largest single companies of Northern Engineering Industries, an important force in the steam generation and power raising industry.

During its history it has achieved a number of outstanding firsts in boiler design. These included the first British boiler of 200 MW capacity at High Marnham, the first 500 MW at West Burton, the first 550 MW at Thorpe Marsh, and the first 375 MW supercritical unit at Drakelow 'C'. It was during this period in the early 1960s that International Combustion was also associated with the successful building and commissioning of the first 500 MW nuclear power station at Trawsfynydd.

The Derby Works was initially developed over 55 acres in Sinfin Lane on the southern outskirts of Derby to provide engineering works for the Underfeed Stoker Company, who transferred its operations from Newark in September 1922.

In 1923, at Barrow-in-Furness, a company was formed under the names of Vickers and International Combustion Engineering Limited which was a joint venture between Vickers Limited and the Combustion Engineering Corporation of New York. It undertook to manufacture and sell under licence within the United Kingdom a new method of firing large boilers — pulverised fuel firing. Eventually it was to undertake the complete design of boiler plant and much of the ancillary equipment. Two years later, in 1925, Vickers withdrew from the venture and the name was changed to International Combustion.

With orders increasing, International Combustion needed to expand its manufacturing capacity. This was to prove impractical at Barrow and a decision was taken to move to the Derby Works — at the time only partly developed. The move took place in 1928, following an extensive building programme and, in 1931, the drawing office and design engineers, then situated in London, were moved to Derby, thereby centralising the manufacturing and designing staffs.

Between 1928 and 1934 there was a substantial

grouping of a number of companies associated with boiler plant. Finally, in 1934, the New York influence was bought out and these associated companies went public and began trading under the single title of International Combustion Limited, operating entirely on British capital. During World War Two, the company was engaged in the production of boiler plant for Corvettes, torpedos, hand grenades and a variety of other war equipment requirements.

By 1950, International Combustion (Holdings) Ltd had been created acting as a parent company for a rapidly growing group, and since then many other engineering companies have become part of the group.

In April 1989, Rolls-Royce and NEI reached agreement on the terms of a merger. During 1990, Rolls-Royce announced a major change in structure since the merger with NEI with the creation of the Aerospace Group and Industrial Power Group, which includes NEI.

The company name changed to International Combustion Limited, part of the Rolls-Royce Industrial Power Group, with effect from 1 February 1993.

F.W.Hampshire & Co Ltd, Manufacturing Chemists

THE first factory of F.W.Hampshire's was situated in the Riverside Works in the Old Silk Mill in Derby, and cough mixture, sticky fly-papers ('Wasp Fly Bands') and various food products were manufactured there. In 1910 a disastrous fire completely destroyed all stocks of materials and machinery.

Although production was restored in other premises, it was in 1929 that Hampshires moved into the new purpose-built factory and offices, known as Sunnydale Works, in Sinfin Lane. In the period up to the war they continued to manufacture Zubes Cough Sweets, sold in small round tins, and the Keybells range of Cough Mixtures, 2d (old money) for a small bottle, and Keybells Liver Salts. Many people will remember the famous spotted horse, which appeared on hoardings around the country, with its slogan: 'Hoarse? Go Suck a Zube'. Other food products included Creamilla and Luxona Ice-Cream Powder, Sundilla Ice-Cream Wafers and Egrol Custard Powder. Another of their well-known lines was the Snowfire range which included ointment, cold cream and face powder at very reasonable prices. All the boxes and tins used for the products were made on the premises.

In the 1920s, there were 60 representatives working the country. Stock was also sent to premises in Dublin. Eventually a factory was opened in Dublin which produced the Pomeroy luxury cosmetic range, and one of the employees from Derby went over to manage it. Goods were exported from Derby to Canada, Australia and New Zealand.

Among the people with senior positions in the firm were Mr Moseley (chairman and managing director), Mr Watkin, Mr Weaver, Mr Harry Cawdron, Mrs Wilford (secretary), and the chemist, Mr Lander.

The wartime restrictions must have caused many

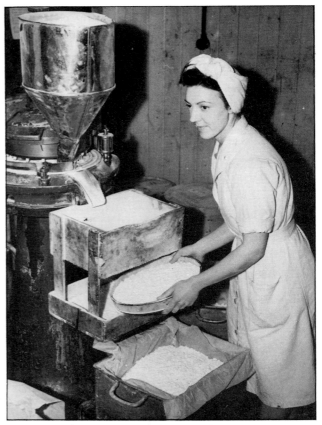

Sugar coating Zubes at F.W.Hampshire's.

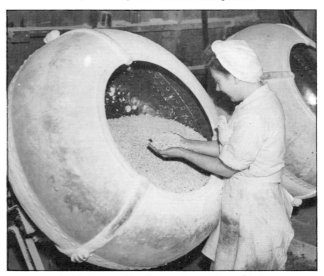

Tableting machine for asprins at Hampshire's.

problems for the company, but they continued to provide employment for many women and girls from the surrounding area, including work on machines installed to produce small-arms ammunition.

In 1965, Hampshires became part of the Reckitt & Colman Group, and is now part of Reckitt & Colman European Manufacturing. There are two units on the site, one of which produces aerosols and other high volume liquids. Current products include the Haze air freshener range, Mr Sheen, Windolene, Harpic, Dettox etc., which are also produced for Europe.

White Bros (Derby) Ltd, Soft Drinks Manufacturers

IN 1898 two brothers who were tenant farmers on

Horse-drawn White's delivery cart.

Lord Derby's estate in Bury, Lancashire — Mr Edwin White and Mr James G.White — thought they could better themselves by buying a small business in the Midlands. They therefore drove their horses from Bury to Wolverhampton and started to brew and sell such drinks as herbs and sarsaparilla, ginger beer and hop ale. They used the horses and drays to deliver the drinks in half-gallon stone jars direct to the families who lived in the houses around their factory.

A year later they were joined by their two other brothers, Fred White and Harry White, and the business was so successful that by 1901 they had opened a factory in Birmingham. Another was started in Leicester in 1902, and by 1903 it was decided to expand to Derby, so they invited their cousin Austin Birch — who had been a journalist with the *Bury Times* and the *Rochdale Observer* — to join them in this venture.

Austin Birch found some three-year-old premises in Havelock Road, Derby, which had been a joiner's yard for Smart & Elsom. The business started on 23 March 1903 and by early 1904, Austin Birch was joined by his brother-in-law, James H.Beetham, who had been a master plumber in Bury.

In 1905, Austin Birch moved to London to start a similar business, leaving Jim Beetham as partner in charge of Derby. The photograph taken in the yard at Havelock Road shows that the price of the half-gallon jars about this time was 3d (Jim Beetham is standing by the horse). By 1913, Edwin and Jim White had moved to Birmingham to start the Midland

Counties Dairy, which was sold to Unigate in 1964.

After World War One, only the Wolverhampton and Derby factories remained as botanical breweries whilst the Whites pursued their interests in milk and ice-cream using the Birmingham premises. The first motor vehicle used by the firm in Derby was a Ford 1-ton lorry and this was purchased in 1924 for £140.

Jim Beetham was joined in 1925 by his younger son, J.Herbert Beetham, and during the 1930s the delivery fleet consisted of two Ford trucks and eight horses and drays. The year 1937 saw the introduction of carbonated drinks in glass bottles to supplement the continued success of the stone jar trade.

Running the business became difficult in the early years of World War Two as employees were being called up for war service. In 1942, Herbert Beetham himself was called up into the Burton Fire Brigade and his wife, Maude, ran the business until 1943 when it had to close under the Soft Drinks Wartime Regulations which permitted only one soft drinks factory in a town. Burrows & Sturgess of Ashbourne Road took precedence on account of their size. But there was a method of pooling profits so that those companies which were required to close shared in the profits of those that continued to operate. During this period, the Havelock Road property was used by the Army for the storage of tank parts and also as the ARP post for the area.

In 1946, the business opened up again and Herbert Beetham took the opportunity to change completely to glass bottles and the carbonated soft drinks trade.

White's Morrison electric van, c.1947.

Stone jars were discontinued and many of these bottles were retained by customers for use as hot-water bottles. At this stage the company had no customers, vehicles or staff and the first employees started canvassing for fresh customers in the streets around the factory. Motor vehicles were in very short supply after the war, so four Morrison Electric vehicles were purchased — even though they were limited to 30 miles on one charge.

During the 1950s, the Whites finally withdrew from the Derby business, leaving the Beetham family in full control. Jim Beetham died in 1957 and, in 1959, Herbert Beetham was joined by his son Philip J.Beetham after he had qualified as a chartered accountant.

It is interesting to note that Herbert Beetham's out-of-business activity of playing billiards culminated in 1960 in his becoming English Amateur Billiards Champion, and later that year he went on to become World Amateur Billiards Champion (see *Some Normanton Personalities*).

In the 1960s following the closure of the Wolverhampton factory, Derby was left as the sole survivor of the Whites' original businesses, and the firm continued to keep pace with modern developments in the soft drinks trade.

Garage space became a problem in 1972 when they had 18 Austin Morris vans, and in 1976 the company was fortunate in being able to purchase adjoining property with an entrance in Cameron Road. These premises had been built in 1938 for the Pride of the Peak bus company who later sold to Mansfield & Dawson, a haulage company. On the nationalisation of transport, British Road Services took over the premises, but when denationalised, Porters, the corn merchants, acquired the property. They eventually sold the premises to Stevens, the corn merchants of Shardlow, who renamed the property 'Cameron Mills'.

The 1990s saw the impact of EEC legislation on such things as food standards, weights & measures and labelling. There were inspectors for health & safety, Wages, VAT, PAYE, motor vehicles and the like, none of which the original founders of the business had to contend with. It is hard to think that in the early days, the Whites did not label the bottles but tied different coloured ribbon around the necks to distinguish the variety. Nevertheless, the company is still continuing to produce high quality soft drinks from the same factory in Havelock Road and giving a first-class delivery service using its 14 Sherpa vans. It is looking forward to its Centenary in 2003.

W.W.Winter Ltd

MANY of the early photographs of Old Normanton were the work of the well-known Derby photographers, W.W.Winter Ltd. What may be less well-known is that the firm eventually came into the

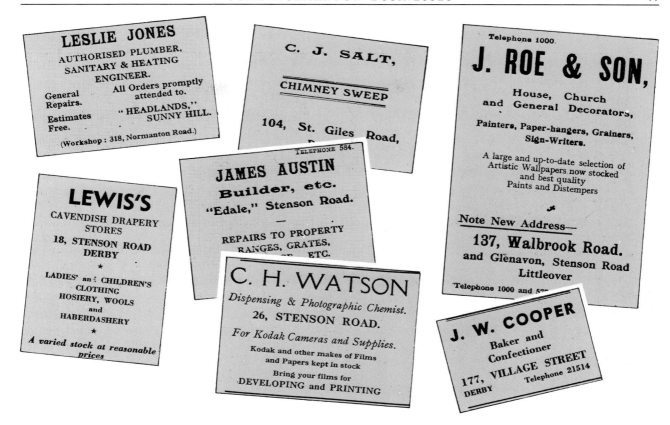

ownership of a Normanton family, the Kings.

The business was founded in Midland Road, Derby, c.1857 by E.N.Charles, who employed W.W.Winter as his assistant. After the death of E.N.Charles in 1864, Winter acquired the business and relocated it in a new purpose-built studio on the opposite side of Midland Road.

In 1896, W.H.King, whose family lived in Normanton, joined the business as photographic assistant, operator and retoucher, and ultimately became the owner.

The business has remained in the family and Hubert King, W.H.King's grandson, became the managing director in 1975. He has long associations with Normanton.

Birds the Confectioners

Birds the Confectioners came into existence in 1919 — just after World War One. Brothers Frank, Reg and Tom Bird pooled their gratuity and with some help from the bank, amassed the £1,000 needed to purchase the business of Peach's, the pork butchers and bakery at The Cavendish. Two of the three owners were confectioners and one was a butcher and together they launched the now famous Birds bread, cakes and pork pies.

Working nearly all round the clock was essential for the brothers and their three employees in those early years. Within eight years, their second shop was opened on Normanton Road with others in the area following.

Queues were a feature of the street scene close to a Birds' shop around this time and with the rationing and restrictions of World War Two, the queues became longer. The high standards first set by the firm were not relaxed and the customers were grateful to enrich their diet with food reminiscent of the quality they had come to expect prior to the war.

The slogan 'We never sell a stale cake' was to be seen on all of Birds' delivery vans and carry-home boxes. Another distinctive feature was the special ribbon used around the boxes to tie them up and which was looped to form a handle.

Frank Bird died in 1951 — he was the last of the founder members. However, the business continued to thrive under the management of Reg and Paul Bird — sons of two of the founders. Paul's interest in the company began when he was six years old — he started working in the cellars at the St James' Street shop putting up customers orders.

The year 1961 again saw rapid expansion. More and more shops were opened — in the centre of Nottingham and towns in between and in the newly expanding suburbs of Derby such as Allestree and Mackworth. The increasing demand which resulted from the increase in outlets led to a search for new and larger premises. In 1971, the company moved to a purpose-built factory on Ascot Drive — built at a cost of £1.4 million.

The original premises at The Cavendish were demolished and a petrol station and workshop facilities were erected on the site.

In 1972, Birds' had 18 retail shops and employed 300 people. Well over 100 lines are made daily and some of the recipes have remained unchanged over the years.

Mr Paul Bird died early in April 1992 — being survived by his wife and his five children. By this time, the company had two bakeries and 38 retail outlets and it was recorded that 26,000 small farmhouse loaves were sold through Birds shops in the city of Derby every week.

Some Normanton Personalities

Lt-General The Rt Hon Sir Frederick Shaw

Frederick Charles Shaw was born on 31 July 1861, the second son of John Shaw of Normanton House, and was educated at Repton. From the Third Battalion (Militia) of the West Yorkshire Regiment, he then secured a commission in the Second Battalion, Sherwood Foresters — the Derbyshire Regiment — in 1882. The battalion was then quartered in Gibraltar and was included in the force sent to Egypt for the operations against Arabi Pasha. Shaw as a lieutenant became signalling officer when the regiment moved to India. Promoted to captain in 1889, he was the adjutant of the Third Battalion for the next five years. He then rejoined his old battalion at Sitapur and Benares. In 1897, Captain Shaw was employed on the staff of Lieutenant-General Sir Baker Russell, commanding the forces in Bengal, but in 1898 he joined the First Battalion and returned to Malta.

During the serious troubles which had arisen in Crete in the winter of 1888-89, Shaw was employed under the High Commissioner. In October 1899 he was promoted to major and went with the First Battalion Sherwood Foresters to South Africa. As brigade major of 21st Brigade, he took part in the march to Pretoria, being present at the actions of Vet River and Zand River. He was at the battle of Diamond Hill in June and at the Wittebergen and Ladybrand operations later that year. As AAG in 1901 until October 1902, he remained in South Africa, and for his services was twice mentioned in dispatches, and made a brevet Lieutenant-Colonel. He was given another brevet in 1906, and a year later, on promotion, took command of the Second Battalion, The Sherwood Foresters. In March 1911 he was appointed GSO 1, Scottish Command, and promoted to the rank of substantive Colonel.

In May 1913, Shaw received command of the 9th Infantry Brigade and took it to France in August 1914 in the Third Division of the British Expeditionary Force. At Mons he held the western side of the salient; at Le Cateau he covered the Divisional retreat after extricating the Brigade from the battle with surprisingly little loss. At the Marne he handled his advance guard in the passage of the river with energy and skill. In October, his brigade saw fierce fighting at Neuve Chapelle during the battle of La Bassee. On 1 November, his Brigade delivered a counter-attack to support the cavalry on Messina Ridge. On 11 November, when the Germans were decisively repulsed near the Menin Road, Shaw was wounded.

For his services in the field he was promoted to Major-General in December. In 1915 he was transferred to the 13th Division which was part of the reinforcements for the operations at Gallipoli. In September, an attack of dysentry meant a return home, and he was appointed Director of Home Defence at the War Office, and in 1916 he became Major-General General Staff, Home Forces, under Lord French at the Horse Guards. In supervising the newly constituted aerial defences of Great Britain, he was involved in a totally new aspect of modern warfare.

At the request of Lord French, the new Viceroy of Ireland, he was made Commander-in-Chief in Ireland and sworn-in as a member of the Irish Privy Council, and was promoted to Lieutenant-General in June 1919. He had been created a Commander of the Bath in 1913 and received his knighthood as KCB in 1917, and he held a number of foreign orders and decorations.

In 1892, he had married Florence Edith, daughter of the Revd John Denton, vicar of Ashby-de-la-Zouch and canon of Peterborough. Her sudden death in Ireland in 1918, when she fell out of a window in Dublin Castle, was a terrible blow to him. Her memorial is in Normanton Church.

In 1922, he unveiled the War Memorial outside Normanton Parish Church and administered the trust set up for Normanton House until it was sold.

In retirement, he lived near Chichester, Sussex. He died on 6 January 1942 at Osborne House, Isle of Wight, in the hospital for retired officers which Queen Victoria had established in part of the house.

NB These notes were provided by Michael Shaw of Winchelsea, East Sussex, great-grandson of John Shaw of Normanton House.

John Shaw of Normanton House

A notable resident of Normanton in Victorian and Edwardian days was John Shaw, who lived at Normanton House from 1873-1906. John Shaw was born at Rosliston, near Burton upon Trent, in 1825, the son of Joseph Shaw, a timber merchant and cooper, and sometime landlord of the Bull's Head in that village. He trained as a surveyor and in the era of rapid railway expansion, took part in railway surveys, and was also involved in various Enclosure Acts which resulted in the large open fields, dating from medieval times, being converted to smaller enclosures bounded by hedgerows. He was also engaged in parliamentary work and as an arbitrator.

John Shaw of Normanton House.

John Shaw commenced business as a surveyor and land agent in Derby in 1848, first in St Mary's Gate and later in College Place, near All Saints' Church. In 1900 he was elected president of the Surveyors' Institute, now the Royal Institution of Chartered Surveyors. He was land agent to first Sir John, and later Sir Vauncey Harpur Crewe of Calke Abbey, the largest landowners in South Derbyshire. In 1887, acting for Sir Vauncey and other landowners adjoining the River Trent, he played an important part in the defeat of the Upper Trent Navigation Bill which would have granted powers for steam navigation in the river from Burton upon Trent to Shardlow.

At Normanton, John Shaw took a leading part in the religious and social life of the village. He was a great benefactor to Normanton and played a large part in the parish becoming an independent benefice. He was churchwarden, and the first chairman of the Parish Council when these were formed in 1894. The old school in Village Street was built by him and given for use as a Sunday School.

Living at Normanton House, the largest house in the parish, he was regarded as squire of the village. The Shaws lived in style, and the women who lived in the village curtsied to Mrs Shaw when they met her in the street. John Shaw died in 1906 and is buried in the churchyard.

One of his sons, Frederick, had a distinguished military career.

Captain Bennett

Captain Bennett, or 'CJ' as he was often known, was a familiar figure in Normanton where he was Scout Master of the 4th Derwent troop.

He was born c.1875, the son of the Revd Norman and Mrs Bennett, and his family home was Bennetstone Hall, near Chapel-en-le-Frith. He served as a trooper in the Boer War and in a Yeomanry unit during World War One when he gained his rank as captain.

In 1908, Captain Bennett was living at Barrow-on-Trent and about this time he started the Barrow scout troop. This was at the very beginning of scouting before it was established as an association in its own right.

He moved to Derby in 1910 and the following year took on the leadership of the 4th Derwent troop when Douglas Foxwell, who had founded it, moved away. The Derwents started up in November 1908, in All Saints' Church House, Full Street, Derby. (All Saints' subsequently becoming Derby Cathedral.) The grounds went down to the River Derwent — hence the name.

The 4th Derwent troop moved their meeting place a number of times in the 1920s until finally coming to the development area of Normanton-by-Derby around 1926-28. Captain Bennett was then living at Normanton Cottage, near the Norman Arms. The orchard belonging to the cottage was often used for camping and a scout from those days, Joe Cooper, remembered spending most of the summer there many years ago and 'CJ's man bossing the boys about'.

At about this time Captain Bennett was personnel manager at Leys Malleable Castings and he also produced their pantomimes.

Normanton Cottage, along with Lake House, disappeared in the 1930s. In 1941 after various moves he finally went to live in the Scout HQ, Derwent Hall, at the top of Coleridge Street, where a local scout acted as his 'batman' — preparing baths in a tin bath and fetching meals from a nearby house. He lived there until his death in 1958.

He was still camping in 1950-52 and many scouting activities are still remembered such as trek camps, visits to France, harvest camping in the 1940s, hikes and camps at Sandybrook Hall, Mackworth, etc., wide games, Jamborees, shows and pantomimes, and the building of Derwent Hall by parents and boys.

During World War Two, when nearing 70, he helped to form and run the Home Guard unit which met in Derwent Hall. They had an indoor rifle range and conducted exercises on Sinfin Moor.

VE Day (Victory in Europe) was celebrated in camp with a bonfire. VJ Day (Victory in Japan) was soon followed by Guy Fawkes Night, 5 November, and there was a great celebration at HQ with a 25ft high bonfire which had a couple of pounds of gunpowder, somehow obtained by 'CJ', in a biscuit tin under the Guy at the top!

Captain Bennett is acknowledged to have been a great influence on the lives of very many of those who knew him in the Scouting movement. He was, without doubt, an archetypal scout, full of adventurous spirit, even at an advanced age. Boys respected and sometimes feared him and if his standards were very high, he had their welfare at heart and believed in the scouting method of training. He remained a bachelor, but he could be charming and entertaining and loved to 'jaw' on any topic. A man of deep religious conviction and a churchwarden at St Giles' Church, Normanton-by-Derby, he did his best to impart spiritual training and guidance to his scouts.

Mr Giles Austin

A native of Torquay, Giles Austin moved to Derby in 1890 and became the owner of a high-class grocery business in the Market Place. He was said to be one of the best-known lay churchmen in Derby, being a member of the Church Assembly, the Diocesan Board of Finance and many other church societies, as well as being a supporter of various charitable institutions. By 1914 he and his family were living in the new house called 'Homelands' which he had built near the Vicarage after purchasing the Normanton House estate previously owned by Mr John Shaw.

At Normanton he became a churchwarden at St Giles' and took a deep interest in all the organisations. He was known for his generosity and is remembered by the gift of land for a new Sunday School and Church Hall at the corner of Underhill Avenue and Village Street in 1928. In the mid-1980s this building suffered continued vandalism. It was eventually sold and the money used to extend the accommodation

Mr Giles Austin, tea-tasting.

at the new Church Centre in Village Street. The Arlington View Nursing Home now stands on the site.

At the memorial service following Mr Austin's death in 1929, the vicar, the Revd Robert Price, said Mr Austin was a great force for good in the parish and described him as 'a devout and humble Christian'. He said: "Amidst all the controversy and confusion of the day, the Bible was enough for him."

Miss Gertrude Austin, his younger daughter, was responsible for the young women's Bible Class and a missionary group in the parish. His elder daughter was married to the Revd Maynard, who became Archdeacon of Mombasa.

Homelands House is now part of the Village Community School, formerly Homelands School. The Austin Estate is named after Mr Austin.

The Wright Family

Bagshaw's Directory of 1846 informs us that C.W.and Francis Wright were the principal landowners in Normanton at that time. The Revd Charles Wright was the Vicar of St Peter's Church, Derby, (the mother church of Normanton) from 1834-1847, when he was succeeded by the Revd William Hope. The patrons were himself, Henry, Thomas, Francis and Samuel Wright. The death of the Revd Charles Wright in 1865, owner of the largest portion of Normanton, brought about many changes for it was decided to sell the estate and it was broken up.

Mr Francis Wright of Osmaston, connected with W.Wright & Company, bankers, of Nottingham, and senior partner of the Butterley Iron & Coal Company, purchased the patronage of St Peter's at this time. He was an enthusiastic Christian who took every opportunity to encourage the preaching of the Gospel. It seems he was hopeful that his son, the Revd Henry Wright, secretary of the Church Missionary Society, would succeed Mr Hope and re-evangelise St Peter's, but in the event Mr Hope outlived them both.

It is, perhaps indicative of the influence of the Wright family that the new church at Normanton (1862) was designed by R.Robinson, the pupil and partner of the architect, H.I.Stevens, who designed Osmaston Church and Osmaston Manor.

Mrs Steeples

Mrs Steeples was well-known for her home-made toffee. She always wore black, and lived alone in the cottage at the end of Barley Row near St George's Church.

The toffee was made in a black iron saucepan on an old-fashioned blackleaded grate. Sometimes when the toffee wasn't quite ready or had to cool, callers would sit and chat with Mrs Steeples in the kitchen — and what a dark room it seemed to them.

However, it was toffee well worth waiting for, and children were very impressed to have their half-pennyworth's (old money) in proper square bags — not the ordinary pointed ones. One of her regular customers was a local doctor who called every week for his order.

Mrs Steeples was confirmed late in life in 1939, and lived only a few more years.

The Cooper Family

The Cooper family are particularly remembered for the bakery in Village Street, but when Mr William Cooper came to Normanton in 1882, it was to work as gardener for Mr W.Briggs, solicitor, of Evington House. Later, he worked as gardener at Normanton House, where his wife was head cook, and they lived in Chestnut Cottage (no longer there) on Village Street, near Normanton House.

Before coming to Normanton he had worked at various places including Stanton-by-Bridge and Allestree Hall. He was obviously an expert on orchid growing and his family have his journal entitled *The Orchid Grower's Manual* where he gives detailed information on all aspects of orchid growing.

Eventually Mr Cooper purchased Daniel Morrell's bakery and village shop (established 1857), and adjoining cottages. At that time, the bakery was just around the corner from Village Street in Browning Street, but later the cottages on Village Street were converted into shops and the bakery was established there. Mrs Cooper ran the bakery and shop and was grateful for the advice and help in obtaining stock which Mr Giles Austin gave her in the early days. Mrs Cooper was a very capable woman and when she rode her bicycle along the village she was said to look like a ship in full sail!

When Mr Cooper died, the parish church bell was tolled 69 times — once for each year of his life, as was the custom in those days.

Mr Cooper's son, Leonard, was a joiner by trade. He spent several years in Australia where his sons, Joe and Leslie, and his daughter, Phyllis, were born. He came back to England in 1917 because of failing eyesight and he and his wife joined his mother and eventually took over the bakehouse and shop. Jack, their third son, was born soon after they returned to Normanton.

Mr Leonard Cooper was followed in the business by his eldest son, Joe, who had served a seven-year apprenticeship with Wragg & Hamblin (bakers and confectioners connected with King's Cafe which stood in St Peter's Street in Derby many years ago). Joe took over the bakery, and with his cheerful smile and pleasant manner was popular with all who knew him. Leslie Cooper had the general shop on the corner, and there was a fish and chip shop and also a sweet shop in the same row. Sadly, the bakery closed in 1974. Since then the shops have all been restored to private dwellings.

For many years a loaf provided by Cooper's Bakery and baked in the shape of a sheaf of corn was a feature of the Harvest Festival decorations at St Giles' Church.

James Herbert Beetham

Herbert Beetham was born at 80 Havelock Road, which is the factory house to White Brothers (Derby) Ltd, the family soft drinks business, where he was to work throughout his life. The family moved to

Herbert Beetham, Normanton's own World Billiards Champion.

52 Derby Lane when he was one year old and he moved to Littleover in 1934 after he had married Maude Smith of Walbrook Road. His main claim to fame was that he became World Amateur Billiards champion in 1960.

His prowess at billiards was certainly not the sign of a misspent youth as he did not start playing the game until he was 19. He joined St Thomas' Church Institute, which is now the Pear Tree Community Centre, and by 1931 he was the Derby Institutes Association Billiards champion. The same year, he entered the English Amateur Billiards Championship, which was an event he was to enter every year until 1992. He was runner-up in 1936, losing by only 30 points after 12 hours play, and was runner-up again in 1946, 1952 and 1959. Following the maxim 'If you don't at first succeed try, try again,' he finally became English Amateur champion in 1960. Later that year he went to Edinburgh where he became World Amateur Billiards champion. He was English champion again in 1961 and went to defend his world title in Perth, Australia, in 1962 but was unsuccessful. He was runner-up in 1962, champion again in 1963 and runner-up in 1977, at the age of 68.

Locally he was a member of the St Thomas' Church Institute team of Reg Barber, George Mumby, Herbert Beetham and Billy Keenan which was top of the Derby Institutes 'A' Division Billiards League every year from 1936 until 1960. This was the year that the Institute had to close because the building was wanted for church purposes. The members took over a room in the Sons of Temperance building in Duncan Road and called themselves the Walbrook Institute. The team of Billy Keenan, David Rees, Herbert Beetham, and Gordon Euston, with Ken Maddocks as reserve, continued to dominate the 'A' Billiards League until the Institute finally closed in 1969.

In his later years, Herbert Beetham spent considerable time in the organisation and refereeing of the game through the Derbyshire Billiards and Snooker Association, of which he was a founder member and first president. Many young snooker players from Derbyshire have reached the national scene through encouragement from the Derbyshire Association. It is interesting to note that even after he had turned 80, Herbert Beetham was still representing the county at billiards. Snooker, of course, had become the more popular of the two games with the younger generation.

Ben Robshaw - late of 141 Stenson Road

Ben Robshaw — listed in *Kelly's Directory* for 1935 as a 'rag merchant' was very keen on sport.

He was educated at the Derby Diocesan School and captained the football and swimming teams. When he was 11 he played local league water polo and by 14 was chosen to play for Derby.

During World War One he served on the Western Front for three years and during this time he played football for the Royal Field Artillery in France and Belgium.

He captained the only Derby team to win the Midland Counties Senior Water Polo title and skippered the side that won the North Midlands League Championship. Ben Robshaw was also champion of the River Derwent — a race which is no longer held.

Amongst his other sporting interests he led the old Markeaton Golf Club team and the Derby Rowing Club, Derby Swimming Club and the Derby & District Wednesday Football League. Derbyshire County Cricket Club also had the advantage of his great energy and interest.

However, he will be best remembered as a director of Derby County Football Club and after the 1946 FA Cup Final, when the Rams won the trophy for the only time in their history, he was presented with a film of the Wembley match. Ben Robshaw died in 1956.

Changes in Normanton

UNDOUBTEDLY the biggest change in Normanton over the years has been in the number of people now living in the area. The volume of housing has increased and so has the diversity of the countries of origin of the populace.

The area under consideration is bounded on the northern edge by Walbrook Road, by St Thomas' Road in a southerly direction as far as Pear Tree Crescent, on to Portland Street to Pear Tree Railway Station on Osmaston Park Road. The boundary continues along the Derby-Melbourne-Birmingham railway line, then slightly to the south of Sunny Hill Avenue, across Stenson Road and through the new estate to Rosamund's Ride. The line goes to Warwick Avenue and then down to The Cavendish.

An important change that has taken place over the last ten or so years has been the building of rest homes and accommodation for elderly people. Two such homes have appeared along the lower end of Village Street close to the Sherwood Hotel and another is opposite the Norman Arms — with sister accommodation around the corner in Underhill Avenue on the site of the former St Giles' Church Hall. Holmfield consists of small-sized units suitable for one or two people — available for sale. Normanton Lodge is warden-controlled accommodation. White Gates,

suitably altered and extended, has become the Littleover Nursing Home.

Much new housing development has recently been completed on former allotments behind the Normanton Cemetery on Stenson Road. The old temporary and mostly wooden houses which served as living accommodation on the avenues there were swept away and private housing developers moved in.

Most of the access to this area is via Wellesley Avenue — beside the Sunny Hill Post Office. However, at this point, one of the many streams that are a feature of the locality, emerges. To cope with the vast amount of water collected here, the City Council have recently created a lake and wildlife park with landscaping. An award was presented by the Derbyshire County Council for the tasteful manner in which this had been turned from a rather derelict scene to one of peace and tranquility.

Land at the opposite end of Sunny Hill Avenue, the former Sunny Hill Camp, has been developed for housing and the factory premises formerly occupied by Qualcast Lawnmowers awaits a new owner.

The Normanton Barracks complex has undergone great changes. The area is presently known as Foresters Leisure Park and includes the Oast House

The Oast House, where Normanton Barracks main gate used to be. There is no local connection with brewing, however.

View along Newdigate Street to where the Normanton Barracks once stood.

View of Normanton House in February 1992, now part of the Village Community School.

The Grange in Ingleby Avenue. It became a hotel after being purchased by Offiler's in the 1930s.

hotel and restaurant, the Showcase 11-screen cinema, the Granada Social Club, Superbowl bowling alley and Quasar (a lazer game area). Also sharing the area is a Kentucky Fried Chicken Fast Food restaurant. Still on the site are several of the trees which were behind the entrance gates to the Barracks and part of the wall on Sinfin Lane which surrounded the buildings on the north side. Lower down this road are still to be seen the row of lime trees which acted as one of the boundaries to the very large sports field which was to the east of the administrative blocks.

The yards and stables at the back of the terraced houses on the Cummings Estate now mostly accommodate light industries, *eg* mineral water manufacture, clothing, vehicle engineering, etc. The estate became known as the Cummings Estate after the purchase in 1884, by a Mr Cummings — a Derby solicitor — of the farm of the late Mr Benjamin Edge. The land was bounded by Village Street and what has become St Thomas' Road, Walbrook Road and Brunswick Street. However, by June 1890, his affairs were in the hands of the London Bankruptcy Court, due, it was said, to an unfortunate speculation in the London theatre.

Changes have taken place at other points around the area. One of the larger houses, Park Hill, has become a social club for the employees of the International Combustion nearby. Evington House is also social club. The Knoll has been demolished and a purpose-built residential home for the less able has been established for many years.

Homelands House and Normanton House both belong to the County Council — as part of the Village Community School — which occupies this large site. A new secondary school was built when the Pear Tree Secondary Modern Schools were amalgamated and moved to the new site. Later, the building was incorporated with the Homelands School — on the adjacent site — when comprehensive education took over.

The Grange became an hotel, purchased by the local firm of Offiler's brewery during the 1930s.

Holly Cottage and Laurel Bank on Derby Lane and Barley Row on Village Street still exist much as they did when the Ordnance Survey produced their map of 1882. So does the village school (formerly the Board School) in Browning Street, but the vicarage (built 1878) shown on that map was demolished in 1986 — being replaced by a more compact vicarage built only three feet from an external wall of the old building.

In the years prior to World War Two, the old bakery (Hallsworth's) was demolished and in its place arose the Greyhound public house.

The Norman Arms, close to the other ring-road, was rebuilt in the 1930s with a mock-Tudor façade adding to the character of the street.

In July 1975, Normanton Parochial Church Council purchased a fairly new property — 211 Village Street. By April 1977, the upper floor had been changed into a flat for the curate, and a meeting room was added at right angles and built on land adjacent to the churchyard. This new building was officially opened by a former curate, the Revd Henry Brierley, on 1 May 1977.

As the years progressed, it was felt that curates required more accommodation and a decision was made to return No.211 to a separate house. At the same time, an extension to the Church Centre to create more meeting rooms and new kitchen facilities was drawn up. Building work started on 1 May 1990 and the official opening was performed by a former member of the congregation, the Revd Michael

The Sherwood Forester Hotel in St Thomas' Road.

Petrol station at the Cavendish, where Bird's Bakery once stood.

Walters, on 4 November 1990.

Now the majority of the Parish Church buildings (except for the Vicarage) are together on adjacent sites.

Places of Worship

THERE have been changes, too, in the occupiers of religious buildings in the area. The Congregationalists vacated their premises when they joined to form the United Reformed Church. The church has been refurbished and is now the First United Church of Jesus Christ. What was the old Sunday School belonging to the Parish Church of St Giles' is now the Church of God of Prophecy, with an entrance directly on to the street. St George's Roman Catholic Church was built on a green-field site close to the Cummings Estate.

At the turn of the century, the Methodists moved from Sackville Street to an open-field site on St Thomas' Road, which in more recent times has been extended and remodelled.

The Sons of Temperance Hall on Duncan Road was established around the turn of the century and the majority of the building has recently been taken over by the Sikh Community and its Shri Guri Radvidass Bhawan Temple.

Road Network

ONE of the biggest effects on Old Normanton during the present century must have been the development of what is now referred to as the Ring Road — formerly the Arterial Road. Newdigate Street was extended north-eastwards and named Kenilworth Avenue, resulting in the awkward line of the road at this point. The road, now known as Warwick Avenue, continued past Normanton Park to the junction with Burton Road.

The arrival of the new road virtually cut Village Street into two sections. As time has gone by, it has become increasingly more difficult to cross between the two parts of the street, due to the heavy volume of traffic.

Disruption has more recently (1992-93) been caused as a result of major roadworks to reinforce the A5111 in order to more easily accommodate the weight of traffic (as well as the volume) which currently uses this road.

Supermarket on the site of the former Cavendish Cinema and the Derby Pavilion.

Connected with the increase in the numbers of vehicles passing through the area are the trappings of the modern age associated with transport. During the 1950s/60s, demolition of the Co-operative Society's unwanted stables and coal vehicle depot on Osmaston Park Road took place. The site was taken over by a large oil company and consequently fuel, etc., is now on sale here.

A different oil company has taken over the shop and bakery area formerly occupied by Bird's the Bakers at The Cavendish. Bird's outgrew this site and, as a consequence, in 1971 removed to purpose-built premises on Ascot Drive Industrial Estate.

A problem associated with the increase in the number of vehicles using the roads is the storage of those vehicles when not in use. Many of the houses in the older part of the area were built long before it was essential for each house/plot to include space for a car. A tour around the area today shows the increase in private ownership of motor vehicles.

Public Transport

AS the century progressed and the built-up area increased, the trams and buses constantly extended their routes. For the opening of Normanton Recreation Ground in 1909, a three-minute service of trams from the Royal Hotel stop in Derby, on the circular

Shop at the corner of Village Street and Derby Lane. In the 1940s and '50s it was owned by Mrs Merton.

Normanton Lodge, Stenson Road, on the site of a former large house.

route, was arranged. This service ran through New Normanton, as far as The Cavendish and along Walbrook Road. By 1935, trolley buses were going as far as Browning Circle to serve the newly-opened Austin Estate.

A motor bus service was serving the needs of those living along the Ring Road by 1960 and Stenson Road was on the circular route going on to Blagreaves Lane. By 1974, motor buses had replaced trolley buses on all routes and Browning Circle was no longer the terminus — the service now extended down Coleridge Street on to Sunny Hill Avenue.

After deregulation of bus services in 1986, smaller vehicles were introduced by the employee-owned Derby City Transport Ltd. These facilitated the manipulation of the buses around the streets of the estates of the area, for example, Grange Avenue and Village Street. In 1992, roadworks necessitated the re-routing of the services, due to road closures and limited access.

Shops

As the car has taken over as the family's main form of transport, the use of the local corner shop has decreased. The move towards out of town shopping and Sunday opening has resulted in purchases being made further afield.

Looking around the area today, it is interesting to note the number of former shops which have closed and are now private houses.

All of the Co-operative Society's branches within the area have gone. Their largest shop was at The Cavendish, with the Jubilee Hall above. They had two outlets on Village Street: the one in the lower part — which was acquired by St George's Church — was demolished for car parking close to the club; the shop that was nearer Stenson Road has, for many years, been a doctor's surgery. The Balaclava Road shops are now a furniture store and some of the units at Browning Circle are awaiting new tenants. The shops at the corner of Wellesley Avenue and Stenson Road all have new owners, which include a hairdresser's and a fish and chip shop.

Cooper's Bakery closed in 1974 and that and the adjacent shops — at the corner of Village Street and

the former Cabbage Square — have reverted entirely to cottage accommodation, whereas the house opposite (which originally was the house of the headmaster of the Board School) changed after World War Two to a newspaper shop — presently Messrs Benyon's.

On the other hand, the number of shops on Derby Lane at The Cavendish, and around the corner in Walbrook Road, has increased.

In the streets where the shops have remained, many now dispense different types of goods. What was, for many years, a licenced general shop at the corner of Grange Avenue and Village Street, has recently become, again, a chemist. At the corner of lower Village Street and St Thomas' Road, where at one time was a pawnbrokers, is now a second-hand shop.

There have been changes in the type of goods sold from the group of shops on Newdigate Street: close by, at the corner of Village Street and Sackville Street, the shop here now sells and hires video films. The sweet shop (Sudbury's) which was opposite the entrance to Normanton Barracks on Osmaston Park Road was demolished for road widening, as was Morton's cycle shop which was next door.

Recreation

THE constant building up of the area has led to the loss of many of the open spaces — footpaths which took the users out into the country very quickly and recreational areas such as allotments. To compensate for this, at the beginning of the century, Normanton Recreation Ground was opened, whilst at the other edge of the area, the Sherwood Recreation Ground was made available prior to World War Two. Within the last 20 years, Coleridge Street Park, close up to the Derby-Birmingham railway line, came into use, and in 1987 there was the creation of Sunnydale Wildlife Park off Wellesley Avenue. Seven hectares of overgrown allotments were transformed into an open space for play and leisure whilst preserving and promoting wildlife by diverting a stream into a clay-lined hollow colonised by frogs, newts and several types of fish. The Derbyshire County Council's Greenwatch Award was given to the project in 1992.

Mr Webster of Carnegie Street, at the scene of the demolition of the Co-op stables on Hopetoun Street and Osmaston Park Road, now the site of the Shell filling station.

Looking To The Future

AS we approach the twenty-first century, it is pertinent to wonder how Normanton-by-Derby will look in the future.

Proposals have already been put forward by the City Council to spend large sums of money in this area. It has been suggested that some houses on the Austin Estate might be demolished to make way for modern low-cost housing. The redevelopment of the Sunny Hill Works site (formerly occupied by Qualcast Ltd) with housing, leisure and recreational facilities is a fairly large scheme which is presently under consideration. The revitalising of the Browning Circle shopping area is also being addressed.

As part of the Derby City Challenge, the development of a community refurbishment scheme to help job and training opportunities could start at Kenilworth Avenue from April 1994.

From time to time there have also been suggestions that some of the older housing in the vicinity — which does not come up to present-day standards — should make way for modern properties.

With the increase in leisure activities, will there be greater use made of the many parks and community facilities available in the area? Will there still be the need for allotment gardens?

As we move to the next decade, will there be as much emphasis on private car ownership — or will we be looking for an improved public transport system to conserve fuel and roads?

Will there be as many light engineering type companies carrying on business — or will these be moved to purpose-built complexes on the outskirts of the city. Or could such businesses be resited within the Normanton area?

Normanton St Giles' Orchestra pictured in 1929 outside St Giles' Church.

George Broughton – Stop Me and Buy One

George Broughton and his sister, Daisy, lived in Brunswick Street where their father had a wood-yard. During the 1950s and '60s, George was well known around the streets of Derby as a 'Stop Me and Buy One' ice-cream man. He rode a tricycle with a large box-like container between the two front wheels. Inside this structure, the vanilla ice-cream was stored and kept cool. On top, in large tins, were kept the cornets and ice-cream scoops.

George toured the area, including Normanton Recreation Ground, ringing his hand-bell to attract the attention of customers. It is said he was arrested on a regular basis — for ringing his bell. He sold ice-cream for a local firm — Storer's — and latterly for the national company, Walls. George dressed himself in a navy serge jacket and wore a peaked cap.

Out of season, George delivered firewood on behalf of his family's firm. Broughton's had a woodyard from where they made deliveries to local retail outlets and businesses of sticks for the domestic coal fires. In December, George could be found knocking at doors in the area to take orders for ice-cream cakes for delivery on Christmas Day.

During the 1930s, his father was also well-known in Normanton for his presentation of magic lantern shows — often in the 'Old Sunday School' on Village Street. He was a keen member of the congregation of the Parish Church.

Normanton St Giles' Orchestra

For many years, Normanton St Giles' Orchestra, under their conductor, Mr George Taylor, were responsible for monthly musical services on Sunday afternoons in St Giles' Church. These services were very popular and the collections were given to various charitable organisations and church expenses.

Coxons the Builders

In the 1800s, Coxons the builders of Village Street were associated with the building of Normanton Barracks at the top of Sinfin Lane, and Normanton School and the first Vicarage in Browning Street. Although the family name has died out in Normanton, two of Mr Coxon's great-granddaughters, Mrs Woodward and Mrs Post, still live in the village. Each week a beautiful flower arrangement in a stand given in memory of one of the family, Mr Brian Woodward, gives pleasure to people coming into St Giles' Church.